100 things to do in Niigata Furumachi

新潟古町100選

Furumachi
100s

Sun bread
サンブレッド

Raisin bread
レーズンブレッド

Gorgonzola

Croque monsieur
クロックムッシュ

Contents

Map

Activity

Cafe + Bar

Shopping

Lunch + Dinner

Visit

Introduction はじめに

　この本の舞台は、新潟市の古町エリア。地元の人は「ふ」にアクセントを付けて、この地域を「ふるまち」と呼びます。JR新潟駅から車で5分。景色を楽しみながら歩けば２０分。日本海や信濃川が近く、鉄道駅から少し距離があるのは、新潟が江戸時代から湊町（※）として栄えた証です。そして現在、その湊町の文化が色濃く残る古町には、地域の伝統を受け継いできた老舗やセンスの光る個性豊かな個人店が多く集まっています。

　『新潟古町100選』は、そんな古町をこよなく愛する方々に、普段から通うお店や場所での過ごし方を100個紹介してもらう企画です。紹介してくれるのは、この地で暮らす人や働く人をはじめ、ものづくりや表現に関わるクリエイターや作家、飲食店の店主、行政職員など多種多様。この本を通して、この街を楽しむ方々が織りなすリアルな日常を知り、また古町を訪れる方の手助けとなるようにと願いを込めたローカルガイドブックです。

　『新潟古町100選』が導く新しい出会いや発見を楽しみましょう。

古町セッション 近藤潤

This book is set in the Furumachi area of Niigata city, which is located a mere five-minute drive from JR Niigata station or a pleasant twenty-minute walk. The Sea of Japan and Shinano river are both close nearby. In the Edo period (17th-18th century), Niigata flourished as a port town despite being far from the railroad station. Since then, the traditional culture of that time has been preserved in the Furumachi area, resulting in the presence of several long-established and unique privately-run businesses.

"100 Things to Do in Furumachi" is a collection of recommended places by Furumachi enthusiasts. These recommendations come from a variety of sources, including people who work or live in Furumachi, creators, artists, business owners, and city officials. We hope this book will help you understand the lives of these colorful people and enjoy Furumachi.

Let this book lead you to new discoveries and joyful encounters.

Jun Kondo, Furumachi Session

※ 「港」は船着場のこと、「湊」は港に人やものが集まる場所のこと。
　新潟市では古町エリアのことを湊町と表記します。

About Furumachi 　古町について

　新潟市は、古くから日本海側最大の流通を担う港として栄え、明治初期には開港五港の一つとして開かれました。その中心市街地が現在の古町。湊町として人々に愛されてきた歴史地区にあたります。

　鉄道や車のない時代、船こそが物流のかなめ。町割りは信濃川に沿って弧を描くように道がつくられ、舟による運搬のために堀（水路）が張り巡らされていました。その中でも特に主要だった西堀と東堀は、今でも〝通り〟として残っています（次ページ地図参照）。そして、その二つの堀の間にある商店街が、このエリアの名前の由来である古町通というメインストリートです。

　古町の魅力は、湊町として続く深い歴史や、もてなしの文化、そこから滲み出る街の雰囲気に引き寄せられて集まって来る人々やハイセンスな感性をもつ店主たちです。それを感じるための一番いい方法は、『新潟古町100選』をきっかけに古町を訪れて、店主にこの街のオススメを尋ねてみること。きっと、さらにディープで楽しい古町を教えてもらえるはずです。

Niigata city has flourished as the largest port city on the Sea of Japan coast since ancient times. It was opened as one of the five ports of the Meiji era. The current Furumachi district was the central downtown area at that time.

In the era without railways and cars, ships were the key to logistics. The town was divided into roads that curved along the Shinano River, and canals were built for transportation by boat. Among them, the Nishibori (west canal) and Higashibori (east canal) were particularly important and still remain as streets. The shopping street in between both canals is the main street of the Furumachi area.

The charm of this area lies in its deep history as a port town, its culture of hospitality, and the people with refined sensibilities who are attracted to the atmosphere of the town. The best way to experience the local charm is to visit the Furumachi area and ask shopkeepers for their recommendations, using this book as a starting point. You will be able to learn about even more deep and enjoyable aspects of Furumachi.

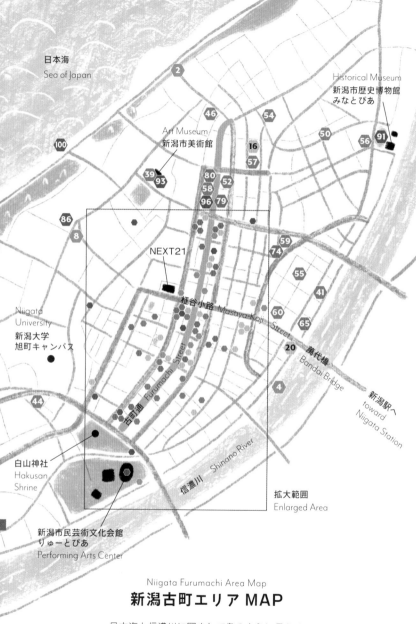

日本海
Sea of Japan

Historical Museum
新潟市歴史博物館
みなとぴあ

Art Museum
新潟市美術館

NEXT21

柾谷小路　Masaya-Koji Street

Niigata
University
新潟大学
旭町キャンパス

古町通　Furumachi Street

萬代橋
Bandai Bridge

新潟駅へ
toward
Niigata Station

白山神社
Hakusan
Shrine

信濃川　Shinano River

拡大範囲
Enlarged Area

新潟市民芸術文化会館
りゅーとぴあ
Performing Arts Center

Niigata Furumachi Area Map

新潟古町エリア MAP

日本海と信濃川に囲まれて島のように見える
通称 "新潟島" の中心市街地です。

（2023 年 12 月時点の位置情報）

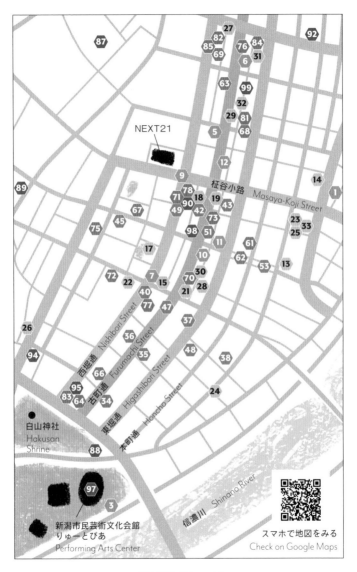

NEXT21

柾谷小路 Masaya-Koji Street

白山神社
Hakusan
Shrine

新潟市民芸術文化会館
りゅーとぴあ
Performing Arts Center

西堀通 Nishibori Street

古町通 Furumachi Street

東堀通 Higashibori Street

本町通 Honcho Street

信濃川 Shinano River

スマホで地図をみる
Check on Google Maps

拡大範囲 Enlarged Area

Map

Activity

この本では「古町の過ごし方」を
5つのカテゴリーに分けて紹介しています。
この本を手にとったあなたは
どのように古町を過ごしたいですか？

1

atori のお弁当を買って やすらぎ堤でランチ

地元農家さんの季節野菜を中心にお弁当をつくる atori さん。野菜の自然の色なのにとっても鮮やかな見た目にワクワク。食べてみると美味しいのはもちろん、いろいろな食感や味を楽しむ事ができて、五感をしっかり使っていただいていることを実感します。歩いて5分のやすらぎ堤で新潟らしい景色を堪能し、ゆったり季節を感じながら食べるのがおすすめです。

Enjoy ATORI's Boxed Lunch

At Yasuragi-tei on the Shinano river bank, you can enjoy Atori's boxed lunch made with local farmers' vegetables. The naturally vibrant colors of the vegetables are a feast for the eyes, and the flavors are guaranteed to tantalize your taste buds. Use your five senses to enjoy different textures of food. It's just a five-minute walk from this shop to Yasuragi-tei, so you can enjoy your lunch on the river bank while feeling the seasons outside.

Activity

小笹教恵｜ヒメミズキ
古町通にて新潟県内外からセレクトした作家ものを取り扱う、うつわギャラリー「ヒメミズキ」を営んでおります。海から吹く風で季節をはっきりと感じ取れる新潟古町が好きです。

② 日和山展望台で日本海の朝焼けを望む

夏の早朝４時頃、眠れずにいると窓越しに格別の色が見えはじめる。日和山展望台で望みたくなり急ぎ自転車で、上り坂必須のため少々息を上げつつ、途中早起きの地域ネコちゃんたち横目に到着。螺旋階段を登り、そこは海と街の境、空と海の大きさや街と空の関係まで一望できるパノラマ。朝焼けに境界が溶ける日もあれば、ピンク、紫、黄色、オレンジ色は日によりけり、曇りや青だけのグラデーションの日があってもまたよし、決まっているのは太陽が登ってくるということ。街を愛おしく見晴らす。

Catch the Sunrise at HIYORIYAMA OBSERVATION DECK

One sleepless early summer morning, I was captivated by the stunning colors of the sky. I hopped on my bike and pedaled up the slope to reach Hiyoriyama Observation Deck. As I climbed the staircase, I was greeted by a panoramic view of the sea and town. The border of the broad sky and sea awaited me, and the morning sun blurred the skyline or reflected the sky in pink, purple, yellow, or orange hues, depending on the day. Whether it's a cloudy or sunny day, you can enjoy various shades of sky at this observation deck. Don't miss out on catching a glimpse of the sunrise over the town!

近藤実可子

某刺繍のひと。作品展出品のほか、刺繍小物の製作販売、刺繍イラストでの挿絵や装丁など幅広く活動している。１２年間育てていただきました、ありがとう古町大好きです。

③ りゅーとぴあの空中庭園で水盤に映る朝日を見る

りゅーとぴあ 新潟市民芸術文化会館。緑あふれる敷地内には屋上の庭園のほか６つの空中庭園と水路や池があります。信濃川の水面と視覚的に連続するように設計されている水盤。やすらぎ堤をランニングした後、その水盤に映る朝日を見て１日を始めるのがおすすめです。水の中に映り込んだもう一つの世界。幻想的な景色を見ているとランニングの疲れも一気に吹き飛びます。

RYUTOPIA'S HANGING GARDEN: Watch the Morning Sun Reflect in the Pool

At Ryutopia Niigata City Performing Art Center, you can find a rooftop garden and six hanging gardens, as well as a canal and ponds. A pool is designed to look connected with the surface of the Shinano river, and the morning sunshine reflecting in the water is fantastic.

小笹教恵 | ヒメミズキ

古町通にて新潟県内外からセレクトした作家ものを取り扱う、うつわギャラリー「ヒメミズキ」を営んでおります。海から吹く風で季節をはっきりと感じ取れる新潟古町が好きです。

やすらぎ堤で
ナイトピクニック

やすらぎ堤でピクニックをするなら、圧倒的に左岸側がおすすめ。なぜなら平地の芝生エリアが広くて、空いているから。万代エリアの夜景を眺めながら、"新潟の台所"本町で調達した竹徳かまぼこさんの海老しんじょうや、ことぶき屋さんの餃子を持ち寄るのが楽しい。おしゃれにワインというより、新潟人なら粋に日本酒で。音楽を流してライトを置いたらそこはもう極上の社交場。

Night Picnic in Niigata at YASURAGI-TEI RIVER BANK and Food From Honcho Food Market

If you're looking for a serene and less crowded spot to enjoy a night picnic in Niigata, the Furumachi side of Yasuragi-tei river bank is an ideal choice. The area boasts a wider green space and offers a breathtaking view of the Bandai area. To make your picnic even more delightful, grab some food from Honcho food market. You can try fish cake from Taketoku fish cake shop or gyoza, Chinese dumplings from Kotobukiya. And when you're in Niigata, don't forget to indulge in sake, which is the local specialty. So, put on some music and lights and enjoy the exquisite social atmosphere of Furumachi side of Yasuragi-tei river bank.

稲葉一樹
古町エリアに住まい、働いている公務員。かっこいい人がたくさんいる古町をもっと知ってもらい、どんどんそういう人が集まるエリアになってほしく微力ながら活動しています。

Activity

5

和 gen で着物レンタルし古町花街で撮影会

古町7番町にある着物屋「和 gen」。着物と聞くと敷居が高いようだけど、とても入りやすいお店。なんか一見雑貨屋さんのような感じ。コロナ禍では高校が修学旅行で和装体験などもしている。そんなお店で着物レンタルし、石畳が美しい「新道」を歩いてみませんか。新道は今も歴史的な料亭建築、置屋建築が建ち並んでいます。気分は古町芸妓ですね。

WAGEN: Rent a Kimono and Enjoy a Photo Shoot in the Furumachi Geisha Quarter.

Wagen is a Kimono shop located on the Furumachi 7th block. Although Kimonos might seem intimidating, this shop welcomes anyone who is interested in trying them out. They carry selected Kimono accessories and offer a unique Kimono wearing experience. Why not rent a Kimono and take a stroll on the stone-paved street in the Furumachi geisha quarter? There you can see historical ryotei and okiya, a traditional restaurant and geisha agency streetscape. You will feel like a real Furumachi Geisha.

須貝秀昭

旧中条町出身。高校の時は古町に遊びに行くのがステイタスだった。今は新潟着物男子部部長として毎週のように着物で古町を飲み歩く。

古町芸妓カルチャーから古町の伝統を感じる

古町芸妓を皆さんご存じですか？芸妓と聞くと経営者や富裕層、会食で利用するイメージがあり、少し身構えてしまいますよね？古町芸妓は新潟の誇る格式ある伝統文化ではありますが、若いからという理由で知らない、利用しないのはもったいない！最近の古町芸妓はイベント出演などで目にする機会が多くあり、実は若い層の利用も増えてきています。若者こそ湊町新潟、そして古町の歴史を感じられる古町芸妓を利用してみませんか？

Experience the Rich Tradition of Furumachi through FURUMACHI GEIGI (Geisha) CULTURE

Have you heard of Furumachi Geigi? You might think Geigi are only for parties with business owners or the wealthy, and it might seem intimidating to you. However, Furumachi Geigi are available for anyone's party, and it would be a shame not to take advantage of this opportunity! Furumachi Geigi often appear at events these days, so more young people are inviting them to their parties as well. Young customers are welcome to experience the history of port city Niigata and the entertainment provided by Furumachi Geigi.

田宮翔
古町を拠点とする NSG グループの愛宕商事株式会社所属。 地域を遊びながら学べるカードゲーム「知域王」を制作。 週末は大体古町で飲んでいる、生粋の古町ウォーカーです。

伊佐クリーニング店でクリーニングの相談をする

今どき珍しい個人のクリーニング屋さんです。店内の内装もレトロおしゃれ。クリーニング後の衣服を保管・管理するためのレールがあるのですが、機械で動きます。それが内装と相まってめちゃくちゃカッコ良いです。仕事もていねいで、急ぎで欲しい時は相談に乗ってくれます。自社で洗濯されているからこそその対応力によく助けられます。

ISA CLEANING SHOP: Get Expert Dry Cleaning Consultation

It's becoming increasingly rare to find independent dry cleaning shops. However, this particular shop stands out with its charming retro interior and an automated hanger rack lane that adds a touch of modernity. The shop offers meticulous work and flexible services, thanks to its in-house workshop.

西山りっく
新潟市のイラストレーター。 古町は中高生の頃からよく通っていて、古着屋さん巡りをしたり映画を見たりしていました。

Activity

8

萬代橋からどっペリ坂まで
サイクリング

新潟市の景観の代表とも言える萬代橋。春は桜を望め、夏は信濃川を流れる心地よい風を感じ、秋は紅葉、冬は河川敷が真っ白に染まる銀世界を堪能することができます。新潟の四季を感じながら、レンタルサイクルでどっペリ坂に向かって走ります。夕方は特におすすめ。自転車で走る目線の先には日本海に沈もうとする夕日を眺めることができます。どっペリ坂に着いたら、少し高い場所に登って来た道を振り返ります。夕日に照らされた金色の新潟の街や萬代橋は新潟市の宝物の一つではないでしょうか。

Cycling from BANDAI BRIDGE to DOPPERI SAKA SLOPE: A Scenic Journey Through Niigata's Four Seasons

Bandai Bridge is an iconic landmark that represents Niigata's cityscape. From here, you can enjoy the gorgeous cherry blossoms in spring, feel the comfortable breeze from the Shinano River, appreciate the autumn-colored leaves, and witness the winter snow-covered river banks. Rent a bike and let it take you on a journey through Niigata's four seasons. We recommend cycling towards Doppperi Saka Slope in Nishi Ohata and ending your bike journey by watching the sunset. When you reach the top of the slope, take a few steps up and look back to see a view of a Niigata city's treasures reflecting the evening sun.

本間亘｜THE COFFEE TABLE
上大川前通で THE COFFEE TABLE というカフェを運営。海と川に囲まれた素晴らしいロケーションが古町の特長の一つだと思っています。

西堀ローサ‐古町モール間を冬ウォーキング

全天候型古町ルフルで集合し、みんなでストレッチ。そして西堀ローサへ。地下街としては日本海側では随一の規模を誇るほど広い。レトロな絵画が描かれた外壁や照明は懐かしくノスタルジックな雰囲気を感じながらウォーキング。その後、連結してあるルフルに戻ってそのまま古町モールへ向かい、ドカベンのキャラクターの銅像が建ち並ぶ「ドカベンロード」を傍目に元気に古町を歩きましょう。往復2キロ近くになります。雨風の影響を受けない屋内で楽しく運動しましょう。

Explore NISHIBORI ROSA and FURUMACHI MALL while Staying Active in Winter

Hang out at the all-weather friendly Furumachi Refuru and stretch your legs. Then, head to the underground Nishibori Rosa mall, which is the longest and widest underground shopping mall among the coastal cities of the Sea of Japan. Enjoy walking around the mall and take in its retro-style decor and lights that create a nostalgic atmosphere. Afterward, you can walk along Furumachi street to the 5th block to reach Dokaben road. Here you'll be greeted by statues of famous Japanese baseball anime character. This course is about two kilometers long, so you can get some exercise under the roof without worrying about the weather.

須貝秀昭

旧中条町出身。高校の時は古町に遊びに行くのがステイタスだった。今は新潟着物男子部部長として毎週のように着物で古町を飲み歩く。

Activity

りゅうと接骨院で
マシンガン治療をしてもらう

研修生の頃からお世話になっている「りゅうと接骨院」。数年前から導入された "ショックマスター" という器具を使った患部に衝撃を当てることで神経に働きかける治療があり、これが身体の痛みにとても効きます。院長の中村先生がダッダッダッ...という軽快な音で治療してくれながら、いろいろ話や悩みも聞いてくれるので、元気を分けてくれます。

RYUTO BONESETTLER CLINIC: Get 'Machine Gun' Treatment

As a trainee of Noism, I received help from the chiropractor at Ryuto Bonesettler Clinic. The recently installed equipment called "shock master" works on the affected part's nerve and effectively treats body pain. The doctor listens well to patients' concerns, thus helping them to feel better.

池ヶ谷奏
コンテンポラリーダンサー兼ダンス講師として新潟と東京の2拠点で活動中。新潟に来た12年前から古町近辺に住んでおり、新しくなっていく店々と変わらない景色を楽しんでいる。

Golden Pigs で多彩な音楽を開拓する

新潟古町エリアにあるライブハウス。ロック、パンク、テクノ、ヒップホップなどさまざまなジャンルのライブを楽しめます！地元のアーティストなども多く出演しているライブハウス、僕も初めて足を運んだのが友人のライブでした。初めて行った時は緊張したなー。ロビーに貼ってあったり、置いてあったりするおびただしい数のフライヤーから気になるものを見つけてきて、聞いてみたり、実際にライブに行ってみたり、知らない音楽を探すのも楽しいです！フライヤーのデザインを見ているだけでも楽しいですしね。

GOLDEN PIGS: Discover a New Genre of Music

Located in the Furumachi area, this small venue offers a variety of music genres such as rock, punk, techno, hip-hop, and more. You can enjoy live shows by local artists. During my first visit, I was excited to see my friend's band perform. The atmosphere was electric! The walls are adorned with numerous flyers that showcase upcoming shows and new bands. It's a great way to discover new kinds of music. The designs of the flyers are also fun to see.

ke-shiki
新潟市北区で木製オリジナル・オーダーの家具と美容室を営む施設を運営。古町は行くたびに新しいモノやコト、ヒトに出会える場所！

RYUTist のホーム・古町へライブを観に行く

古町を拠点に活動している３人組のアイドル。今や古町だけでなく県外でのライブも数多くこなしていて、豪華な楽曲提供やさまざまな新しい企画を行い、常に進化している印象です！古町で定期的にホームライブを開催し、"古町どんどん"にも毎回出演していたりと、地元新潟を大切にしているのが伝わります。RYUTist さんのピュアな人柄、歌声、ダンスなど真っすぐな姿が愛されるアイドルです。

Experience a Live RYUTist Performance in Furumachi

RYUTist is a three-member idol group based in Furumachi, Niigata. They have been active since 2011 and have performed live not only in Furumachi but also in other parts of Japan. They have a strong connection to their home Niigata, as evidenced by their regular home live events in Furumachi and participation in Furumachi Don Don, a seasonal event held in Furumachi. RYUTist's pure personality, singing voice, and dance are endearing. They have released several singles and albums since their debut. Their music is known for its catchy melodies and upbeat rhythms that are sure to get you moving.

ミュミュ
新潟市の美容師。古町で子育てしたり、オタク活動したり、散歩したり、飲みに出かけたり。

Activity

Cafe + Bar

のんびり、ゆったり

13

ナッツ上大川前店で
モーニングセット

午前8時から開店しているナッツ。「いらっしゃいませ〜！」。シャキっとしたあいさつが心地良い。オススメはモーニングセット。ふかふかの食パン、ボリュームたっぷりのポテトサラダ、シャキシャキなキャベツの千切り〜ハムを添えて〜、淹れたてのコーヒーが元気にしてくれる。スタッフのみなさんが仲がよく、その姿はなんだかあたたかい気持ちになる。

NUTS: Start Your Day with a Hearty Breakfast Set

Nuts opens at 8:00 AM and you are welcomed with a cheerful greeting that will make you feel right at home. Their breakfast set is highly recommended and includes fluffy toast, voluminous potato salad, crispy vegetables with ham, and freshly made coffee that will lift your spirits. The staff is friendly and welcoming, which makes for a warm and inviting atmosphere.

高橋紘子
古町に住んで15年。食べて、飲んで、癒されて、私の体は古町でできています。

27

14

ブルーカフェで窓の外の
並木道に季節を感じる

Blue Cafe は古町中心部から少し離れて佇む、いわばオアシス。食事、喫茶、読書、ライブ、ワークショップ等々、過ごし方や活用の仕方はいろいろ。2階の広い窓から、新緑や紅葉、季節の風景をただボーッと眺めて過ごすのも良い。お酒もあるのでハッピーアワーにも良い。常に3～4種類から選べるカレー、大きなマグカップで出てくるコーヒー、チャイがおすすめです。

BLUE CAFE: Seasonal Views Through the Window

Blue Cafe, nestled away from the bustling heart of Furumachi, feels like an oasis. Whether you want to eat, drink, read, attend live shows, or participate in workshops, this cafe caters to your needs. Sit back and enjoy the changing seasons through the window—lush greenery in spring and vibrant leaves in autumn. Their alcoholic beverage selection is sure to satisfy you. Don't miss out on their daily offerings of three to four curry varieties, and consider sipping coffee or chai from their generously sized mugs.

石塚里栄子
趣味のカリグラフィー、刺繍のワークショップをブルーカフェで開いています。

15

カフェ・ド・ダックの
オムライスを食べる

古町にあるカフェ。外に出ている看板はカタカナで"カフェ・ド・ダック"とちょっと気になり入ってみたくなるような看板が印象的です。お店は階段を上って2階。店内は何処となく懐かしい雰囲気。優しいマスターとママの掛け合いが心地よく、いつも落ち着く時間を過ごせています。私のおすすめはオムライスとカツカレー。このほかにも美味しそうなメニューが悩んでしまうくらいあります。一度この空間を味わったらまたきっと行きたくなるはずです。そろそろ私もここのオムライスが食べたくなってきました。

CAFE DE DUCK: Satisfy your hunger with an omelet and rice dish

This cafe is located in Furumachi and has a sign with their name in Katakana that may attract you to enter the shop. The cafe is situated on the second floor and has a nostalgic atmosphere. The kind owners of the shop have a friendly demeanor, making it a pleasant place to spend time. My favorite dishes are the omelet and rice, as well as the curry and rice with cutlet. There are many other delicious foods on the menu as well, which can make it difficult to choose. Once you experience the atmosphere, you will want to come back again. I'm craving their omelet and rice now!

ふく
古町の古着屋で働いています。古町という場所が好きなので、休みの日でもよく散歩に出かけます。出勤前は白山神社に参拝してたから仕事へ行くことも。

16

コンバインドカフェ五徳
屋十兵衛で下町を知る

朝はモーニング。夜はもつ煮で一杯。2階のスタジオでは花魁に変身。海外からもお客さんが来る魅力満載のお店です。コンバインドカフェとは複合型の意。憩いのカフェで読書、レンタサイクルステーション、将棋・麻雀・囲碁倶楽部、レンタルスペース、下町街歩き観光の拠点とさまざま。ペットと一緒に飲食も可。新潟の人情豊かな湊町の歴史を感じることができます。

GOTOKUYA JUBEI: Discover Downtown Charm at This Unique Cafe

Start your day with their hearty breakfast set and indulge in a bowl of Motsu, a flavorful gut stew. On the second floor, their studio offers an Oiran experience, where you can step into the shoes of a traditional Japanese high-end lady of pleasure. Their combined Cafe serves as a multifunctional hub, featuring a Cafe, rent-a-cycle station, shogi and mahjong club, rental space for events, and a spot for leisurely town strolls. Pets are warmly welcomed here. Immerse yourself in Niigata's rich history and connect with its vibrant community in this charming spot.

野澤葉子
萬松堂で本を買い、喫茶マキでランチを食べながら読書。

Cafe + Bar

ジャズ喫茶 スワン でジャズに浸る

新潟のジャズミュージシャンの音楽を聴きながら、美味しいコーヒーや紅茶を何杯でも楽しめるお店。西堀通沿いにあるお店でアクセスもしやすく、気軽に音楽を楽しめます。店内は程よく小さな空間でミュージシャンとの距離もぐっと近く、音楽家たちがお客さんの盛り上がりを感じたときには特別な化学反応が起こることも。世代問わずジャズの美しさや気品を感じられるお店です。

Experience the Best of Jazz Music at JAZZ CAFE SWAN

Experience the Best of Jazz Music at Jazz Cafe Swan. Savor a cup of tea, coffee, or a drink while listening to some of Niigata's greatest jazz talent. The cafe is conveniently located on Nishibori street, making it easy to enjoy a great musical event. The small and intimate venue has a close ambiance that creates a special chemistry between the audience and performers. It's a treat for all who come, young and old alike, to enjoy the beauty and elegance of jazz music at Jazz Cafe Swan.

Mark Marin

カリフォルニア出身のトロンボーン奏者、英語教師。30年以上新潟に在住。アメリカの有名ジャズクラブより新潟のジャズシーンが好き。

喫茶 MAKI でマダムたちの会話に耳を傾ける

Wi-Fiとコンセントがあるからと通いはじめた喫茶MAKI。昭和44年創業。時代時代をずっと見てきた喫茶店です。店内はレトロというだけではなく、ホッと一息つけて心地よい時間を過ごすことができます。さまざまなマダムたちのグループが来店し近況報告をし合ったり、店員さんと仲よく話しているのを心地よいBGMにして、美味しいケーキと紅茶をそばにパソコンを作業しています。

MAKI COFFEE SHOP: Overhear Conversations at the Next Table

MAKI coffee shop offers Wi-Fi and power outlets for your convenience. Established in 1969, this shop has been able to observe many different generations. Its cozy decor makes you feel relaxed during your break time. This is a popular place for ladies to catch up and chat with staff. Their conversations are ear-catching. With your cake and tea, you can work peacefully with your PC.

池ヶ谷奏

コンテンポラリーダンサー兼ダンス講師として新潟と東京の2拠点で活動中。新潟に来た12年前から古町近辺に住んでおり、新しくなっていく店々と変わらない景色を楽しんでいる。

19

パルムで罪悪感の少ない豆カレーをいただく

古町の中で希少になりつつあるレトロ喫茶店。そして秘密基地のような立地。喫煙可であるところも魅力のひとつ。罪悪感の少ない豆カレーがとてもおいしいです。コーヒーのラインナップの充実さはもちろんのこと、コーヒー以外のドリンクメニューも充実しています。

西山りっく
新潟市のイラストレーター。 古町は中高生の頃からよく通っていて、古着屋さん巡りをしたり映画を見たりしていました。

PARME: Savor Healthy Bean Curry (with Less Guilt)

Located in the heart of Furumachi, this retro coffee shop is a hidden gem. Smoking is allowed on the premises. The menu features a variety of coffee options, including espresso, cappuccino, latte, and mocha. In addition to coffee, the shop offers a healthy bean curry that is sure to satisfy your taste buds. The menu also includes other beverages. Come and enjoy a cup of coffee or a meal in this cozy and welcoming environment.

Cafe + Bar

20

ラ・しなので信濃川の流れに癒される

美味しいスイーツとコーヒーで、少しゆっくり静かな時間を過ごしたいときにココはオススメ。ホテルオークラ新潟の２階にあるので信濃川や萬代橋を少し高めの位置から見渡せます。ゆったり穏やかな川の流れを眺めながら、街の真ん中なのに喧騒から解放されるというありがたい場所。ホテルなのでサービスもさりげなく、そしてキチンと行き届いているので気持ちのいい時間を味わうことができます。かつそんなにかしこまらずに気軽に使える感じもいい。近場でちょっと特別感とホッとひと息の時間が叶う場所です。

LA SHINANO: A Place to Comfort Yourself with the Shinano River View

La Shinano is a perfect place to enjoy good sweets and coffee in a slow and tranquil atmosphere. It is located on the 2nd floor of Hotel Okura Niigata, overlooking the Shinano River and Bandai Bridge. Even in the heart of the city, you can keep yourself away from the busy downtown and experience quality time with their good hotel service.

北村美和子｜m.holy
本町５でレディスのセレクトショップを経営。個性的な小さな店が点在する古町が面白いと感じ、迷いなく古町エリアでお店をオープン。

シャモニー古町店で待ち合わせ前に本を読む

古町通のアーケードの中、階段を上がって２階にある昔ながらの喫茶店。店内は落ち着いた雰囲気ですが、赤いベルベットの椅子が目を惹きます。この椅子がとても良い。私のオススメは、シャモニーで待ち合わせをしてだいぶ早めに行き、本を読む事です。珈琲は自家焙煎をされていて、香りもよくとても美味しいです。たまに、カフェカプチーノもオススメです。ホイップクリームにシナモンとココアパウダーそしてシナモンスティック付き。ちょっとリッチな気分です。小腹が空いたらピザトーストも。

Pass the Time by Reading at CHAMONIX Furumachi

Chamonix is an old-fashioned coffee shop located on the second floor of the Furumachi 5th block mall. The red velvet chairs are eye-catching and comfortable. I like to arrive early when meeting with my friends and read while waiting for them. The house-roasted coffee is aromatic and tasty, and I recommend trying the cappuccino for a change. The whipped cream with cinnamon, cocoa powder, and cinnamon stick make me feel rich. If you're hungry, I recommend trying their pizza toast.

野口陽子

上古町 SAN の喫茶 UKIHOSHI で働いています。雪のふるまちで、古町と聞いた事がある様なないような…。新潟に住み始めてからずっと古町が好きです。

Cafe + Bar

22

シュガーコートで愛しの 紅茶と焼菓子をいただく

ここにずっとある、紅茶と焼き菓子の
お店 SugarCOAT。フランスやイギリ
スからやってくるという貴重な茶葉を
何十種類も常備し、さらりと提供して
くれる。定番あり、季節のフルーツの
お菓子も豊富なので、たびたび訪れた
らとっても楽しいと思う。どれも大好
きゆえにおすすめは絞れませぬ・・・
お店の素敵さは入ったら真っ先に感じ
られるし、ひとりでも数人でもよい時
間になる。紅茶や、お菓子を作ること
が心から好きで、植物への愛がのぞけ
ることも魅力に思います。

SUGARCOAT: A Haven for Tea and Baked Sweets

SugarCOAT is a charming tea house that has been serving delightful tea and baked sweets for a long time. They offer a wide variety of tea leaves sourced from England and France, which are served in a casual setting. You can choose from traditional sweets or those made with seasonal fruits, making it the perfect place to visit with friends or by yourself. The owner's passion for tea, baking, and plants is evident in every aspect of the cafe, making it a must-visit destination for anyone who loves tea and sweets.

近藤実可子

某刺繍のひと。作品展出品のほか、刺繍小物の
製作販売、刺繍イラストでの挿絵や装丁など幅
広く活動している。12 年間育てていただきま
した、ありがとう古町大好きです。

23

mahorama で一仕事
手の込んだご飯を頂く

萬代橋の古町側、上大川前通から少し
外れたスモーキーピンクなマンション
にある mahorama。男性でも女性でも
1人でふらっと立ち寄ることができて
美味しいご飯が食べられるお店です。
ご飯も飲み物も一仕事手がこんでいる。
こちらのお店はふっと寄りたくなる魅
力がある。マンションの脇に入り口が
あり、中へ入って窓を眺めると不思議
な浮遊感。その浮遊感が日々繋がって
いる時間や空間から引き離してくれる
のかもしれない。

MAHORAMA: Enjoy carefully made meals

Mahorama is located in a smoky pink colored
condominium building on the Furumachi side
of the Bandai bridge, away from Kami-okawa-
mae street. It's a great place to grab a bite
to eat, and the food and drinks are carefully
prepared. The restaurant has an inviting
atmosphere that makes it hard to resist
walking in. When you enter and look through
the window, you'll get a floating sensation and
feel like you are between worlds.

KOULE

活版印刷の KOULE TYPE、作品制作の
KOULE PAPER を運営。10代後半必死に背
伸びしてして古町にいた大人からカルチャーや
ファッションを勉強させてもらった所。

THE COFFEE TABLE のスイーツとカフェラテ

上大川前通三番町にあるカフェ。オーナーの本間さん含めスタッフの皆さんがつくり出す空間がとても素敵。空間もさることながら、ドリンクとスイーツがどれも美味しい。ドリンクは、カフェラテが特に好き。エスプレッソの苦み、ミルクのまろやかさ、それらが口の中で合わさってすっと消えていく後味は堪らない。自家製スイーツは、季節で変わり、バリエーションが豊富なので、飽きが来ない。自分はキャロットケーキやバナナブレッドが大好き。

THE COFFEE TABLE: Indulge in Homemade Sweets and Cafe Latte

Located on the 3rd block of Kami-okawa-mae street, The Coffee Table is a cozy cafe that offers a delightful experience. The owner, Mr. Honma, and his staff have created a wonderful space that is perfect for relaxing and enjoying a cup of coffee. The atmosphere is warm and inviting, and the drinks and sweets are all excellent. I suggest trying their caffe latte. The bitterness of the espresso blends perfectly with the mild milk, leaving behind an irresistible aftertaste. They also offer a great variety of seasonal homemade sweets that never disappoint. My personal favorites are the carrot cake and banana bread.

堀裕介
新潟市役所職員。出身地の西蒲区中之口を中心にワクワクするエリアを作りたい団体 YAKKOTE としても活動。古町在住で古町 SAN にちょこちょこ出没中。

25

Konkret Coffee+Beer のクラフトビール

フレンドリーな雰囲気と、素敵なお店のデザイン、そして良質な音楽で知られるカフェバーだ。月毎に平日の開店日時が異なる。この店の美味しいチーズケーキやランチなど、いろいろな食べ物は満足度が高いこと間違いなし。ナイトロコーヒー、自家製ソーダとクラフトビールがタップで楽しめる。コーヒーはArtefakt Coffee & Press でローストされたスペシャリティコーヒー。のんびりコーヒーや冷たく冷えたビールを楽しむには、本当に最高な店だ。

KONKRET COFFEE+BEER: Relax and Enjoy Craft Beer

Konkret Coffee+Beer is a cafe-bar known for its friendly atmosphere, excellent design, and cool music. It is open on various weekdays and occasionally on a Saturday. Konkret offers a variety of food such as cheesecake and a lunch menu that is sure to satisfy your taste buds. Nitro coffee, homemade soda, and craft beer are available on tap. The coffee served at Konkret Coffee+Beer is made from specialty coffee beans roasted by Artefakt Coffee & Press. If you are looking for a place to relax and enjoy a cup of coffee or a cold beer, then Konkret Coffee+Beer is the perfect place for you.

Neal Graham
英語教師。古町ファン。

Cafe + Bar

26

BarBookBox STORE で靴を脱いで
カクテルをいただく

僕が古町を客人に案内するときに、い
つも連れて行くのがこの場所である。
店主セレクトの気になる本が販売され、
カクテルなども提供するいわゆるブッ
クバーだが、本以外にも気になる雑貨
や食べ物なども扱っている。靴を脱い
で入る店内は、友人の家にお邪魔する
ようなほっと居心地の良さがあり、と
にかくふらっと立ち寄りたくなる場所
なのだが、僕が何よりも好きなのは、
古いビルの階段を上がっていくと正面
に見えてくる店の小窓の向こうから店
主のジュンコさんがいらっしゃいと出
迎えてくれるあの瞬間なのだ。

**BAR BOOK BOX STORE: Sip Cocktails
Sans Shoes**

Whenever I introduce guests to Furumachi, I
make sure to take them to this charming book
bar. The cozy ambiance, combined with a
carefully curated selection of interesting books
and delightful cocktails, makes it feel like
visiting a friend's house. As I ascend the stairs,
my favorite moment is when the owner and
bartender, Junko, greets us through the small
window.

大沢雄城
古町エリアを拠点に活動する建築家。新潟と横
浜の2拠点で、まちと暮らしに関わるさまざま
なことに取り組む。

スタンドおだけで0次会をして小腹を満たす

その名の通り立ち飲み居酒屋。新潟にはあまりない立ち飲みを体験することができる0次会にちょうどいいお店だ。ただ普通の立ち飲み屋さんと違うのは、すべての料理のクオリティーが抜群に高いこと。店主が手間をかけた美味しいアテがちょうど良いサイズの小皿で提供されるので、胃袋に若干の余裕を残したまま二軒目、三軒目と古町の夜にくり出せます。

STAND ODAKE: A Perfect Standing Bar for a Primer

If you're looking for a casual spot to grab a bite before dinner, Stand Odake is the place to be. This standing bar offers excellent quality food that is served in well-portioned small dishes, leaving enough room for you to enjoy a meal at your next place.

真下恵

元ノイズムダンサー。新潟市内を中心にヨガやバレエ、コンテンポラリーダンスのレッスンを開催。新潟に住み始めて約16年、古町に身も心も捧げております。

Jazz Flash でレコードの音色に酔いしれる

店内の内装はとても個性的で、いたるところにレコードが積み上げられています。ライブイベントで新潟のトップジャズアーティストたちの演奏を聴くと、まるでジャズの歴史に囲まれているような感覚に。さまざまな年代から支持を受けている Flash のステージは、パーフェクトな楽器の音色、心地よい空間、お客さんとの距離感、素晴らしい音響は、お客さんにとってもアーティストにとっても至福の時間を過ごすことができます。

JAZZ FLASH: A Unique Venue for Jazz Lovers

Jazz Flash is a one-of-a-kind venue that offers a unique experience to jazz enthusiasts. The venue is known for its extensive collection of record albums that are stacked throughout the venue. The sense of jazz history surrounds you as you listen to the best jazz artists. The stage at JazzFlash is loved by young and old musicians alike, thanks to its perfect acoustics, comfortable surroundings, closeness with the audience, and that special vibe of the great sound system. The balance of size and sound is exactly what a performance venue should be like. The bar serves tasty drinks while you enjoy great jazz. What else could you want?

Mark Marin

カリフォルニア出身のトロンボーン奏者、英語教師。30年以上新潟に在住。アメリカの有名ジャズクラブより新潟のジャズシーンが好き。

Cafe + Bar

non- でナチュラルワイン と会話を楽しむ

ナチュラルワインとチーズ、県内外の
有名店のお料理も食べられるお店。ワ
インセラーにずらりと並んだワインは
見ているだけでワクワク。内装もおしゃ
れで、古町で飲んでいるなら2軒目は
絶対ここに。店員さんからおすすめの
ワインとお料理を聞いて、お話ししな
がら美味しいナチュラルワインを飲む
のが最高。隣のお客さんと会話になる
ことも多くて、いろんな出会いとつな
がりが生まれるお店。

NON-: Experience Great Natural Wine and Food

Enjoy natural cheese, natural wine, and
famous restaurant food from outside Niigata.
The wine cellar is stocked with an exciting
selection of bottles. This neat and stylish shop
is a perfect place for your second party or to
unwind and enjoy the company of others while
savoring the staff-recommended wine and
food.

星山充子

新潟市でグラフィックデザイナーをしています。
たまにステンドグラスで花器やオーナメント、
鏡なども作っています。古町でお散歩するのも、
飲みに行くのも大好きです!

(30)

Bar Hallelujah で音楽とクラフトジンを語らう

古町モール5の細い路地沿いにある Bar hallelujah。音楽に精通した店主タローさん（本名はまた別。笑）との会話が好きなオトナたちが集う店。長年古町で店を営んでいたタローさんが仕事の関係でハワイへ行き、数年新潟を離れていたときはこれからどこで夜の一杯の時間を過ごせばいいのかと Hallelujah 難民が古町界隈にたくさんいたという話も。手作りのソーセージやミネストローネも絶品。良さを感じてもらうには実際に勇気を持って Hallelujah のドアを開けてみてください。

BAR HALLELUJAH: A Place to Enjoy Craft Gin and Music

Bar Hallelujah is located in an alley on the 5th block of Furumachi. It is a perfect place for people who enjoy conversation with music lover owner, Taro. Homemade sausage and minestrone are some of the best dishes served here. Take a chance and open the door to discover Hallelujah.

北村美和子 | m.holy

本町5でレディスのセレクトショップを経営。個性的な小さな店が点在する古町が面白いと感じ、迷いなく古町エリアでお店をオープン。

Cafe + Bar

31

オーセンティックバー Bar FARO へ立ち寄る

湊町新潟らしい小路で明かりを灯す「灯台」という名前のオーセンティックバーBar FARO。バーがはじめての方から百戦錬磨の方まで、訪れる方に細やかで心地よいサービスで迎えてくれるお店です。果物の旬ごとに多彩な美しさを楽しめる季節のカクテルや、それぞれの個性をていねいに伝えてくれるお酒たちがずらりと並びます。

豊島淳子｜BarBookBox
東中通にあるトールビル3階でBook Bar + Shop「BarBookBox STORE」を経営。古町8番町の洋酒バー カマラードが修行先。

Chill at the authentic bar, BAR FARO

Bar Faro is a sophisticated bar that welcomes both first-time and regular patrons. The bar's name "FARO" means lighthouse in English. Seasonal fruit cocktails are recommended. You can feel comfortable with their professional service.

32

Bar 町田で豊富なオリジナルカクテルを頼む

はしご酒の最後に訪れるのが、Bar 町田。古民家を改装した店内は歴史とモダンが融合していて、どこか安心感があり、入り口は引き戸で靴を脱いであがるのも特徴的。とにかくカクテルの種類が豊富で、干支や星座、誕生花がコンセプトのオリジナルカクテルを頼んでみるのもオススメ。バーカウンターでは、紳士で優しい笑顔のマスターとの会話ができます。古町でゆったりと過ごしたい、そんな日に。

BAR MACHIDA: Sip on original cocktails

End your pub crawl at Bar Machida, a renovated traditional Japanese house with a modern twist that will make you feel right at home. Upon entering, remove your shoes and slide open the door to reveal a wide range of cocktails. Ordering their original cocktails inspired by the zodiac, horoscope signs, or birthday flowers is a fun way to add some excitement to your night. The kind and gentlemanly bartender is sure to amuse you with his conversation. If you're looking for a place to spend a mellow day in Furumachi, Bar Machida is the perfect spot.

平松世梨亜
古町（しもまち）出身。東京から新潟へ拠点を移し、まちに関する活動を行なっているクリエイティブディレクター。古町が大好き。

ニュースナック四ツ目長屋
でサブカル界へ没入

「夜行性の古本屋」と自称し、夜な夜な古町の街角に明かりがともる、なんとも不思議なバー（スナック？）、もとい古本屋である。怪しげにミラーボールが回る店内には、所狭しとオカルトやサブカルなどのこれまた怪しげな本が並び、奥のカウンターではマスターと客がいつでも楽しげに酒を酌み交わしている。このマスターの凄いところはどんなに酔っ払っていても彼のもとへ本を持っていくと内容と魅力をさらっと語れるところである。彼の本とカルチャーへの愛が古町人に愛される由縁なのである。

NEW SNACK YOTSUME NAGAYA: Dive into Subcultural Delights

Nestled in Furumachi, this mysterious bar and used book store comes alive after dark. The ceiling is adorned with a glittering mirror ball, and shelves overflow with bizarre occult and sub-culture books. At the corner counter, the shop's master engages in casual conversations with patrons while sipping his drink. His passion for books and culture continues to draw Furumachi enthusiasts to this unique establishment.

大沢雄城
古町エリアを拠点に活動する建築家。新潟と横浜の2拠点で、まちと暮らしに関わるさまざまなことに取り組む。

Cafe + Bar

幸子さんの古町懐古。

新潟を代表する歌手の小林幸子さん。
古町エリアのお隣・横七番町で生まれた幸子さん
はスカウトを受けて10歳でデビューするまでを
この地で過ごしたそう。今回、『新潟古町100選』
の取り組みに共感してくださった幸子さんに古町
についてお聞きしました。

幸子さんの古町の思い出といえば？

そうね。古町といえば、キラキラとし
た夢のような街でね。両親は横七番町
で精肉店を営んでいて忙しかったから、
隣町の古町へ行く日を指折り数えて楽
しみにしていました。当時は「小林百
貨店」や「大和デパート」があってね。
両親に連れていってもらってデパート
の屋上で遊んだり大食堂で賑やかに食
事したり。「みかづき」は今はイタリア
ンが有名なの？　私の頃はまだそんな
のなくて、「みかづき」と言ったら何よ
り、あのホットケーキですよ。姉妹そ
ろって、初めて食べたホットケーキの
美味しさったら、この世で一番と思っ
たわ。

夢のような場所、いいですね！

**幸子さんは幼少期、どんなふうに過ごされ
たのでしょうか。**

私の実家のお隣が「智泉院」というお
寺でね、小さい頃は毎日のようにお堂
で遊ばせてもらっていました。スカウ
トを受けてデビューすることになり上
京したので、9歳までは栄小学校に通っ
ていました。今でも、同級生から「さっ
ちゃん、元気かー？」と電話が来るのよ。

智泉院

そうそう、曙公園ってまだあるわよね？土俵のある公園。実はあそこ、私が人生初めて大勢の人の前で歌を歌った場所なの。うちの父が「幸子、曙公園でのど自慢大会があるから」って言っておもしろがって、大人しか参加できない大会にヒョイっと上がらせてもらって、畠山みどりさんの歌を歌ったの。そしたら、優勝しちゃったのよ！大人の出場者を差し置いて優勝してしまったものだから「さっちゃんには、特別賞あげるわね」って。ものすごい人だかりの中で歌ったことをよく覚えています。

曙公園

なんと、デビュー戦が曙公園だったとは。幸子さんは、古町をどんな場所だと思いますか？

古町って、すごくロマンティックな名前だと思うの。街並みは新しく変わっているけれど、柳や日本海の風景は変わらずあるでしょう？やっぱり歴史があって、先人の築いてきた土から湧き上がってくるエネルギーというのかしら、まちの香りだったりね。美しい浜辺や日本海に沈む夕陽も、脳裏にあって忘れません。それに萬代橋だって、ものすごいわよ。昔の人があんなに強度のある橋を人の手だけで造っちゃうんだから、パワーを感じるものね。誇らしく思える風景があるって、素敵なことですよね。

幸子さんが今、新潟で取り組んでいることがあると伺いました。

「幸せプロジェクト」という、新潟のお米の自給率を上げていこう、新潟の農業を元気にしていこうと始めた取り組みで、山古志村と津南町でお米を育てています。後継者不足だったり問題も山積みですが、なんと言っても、行動していかなくちゃいけないですからね。お米を中心に一生懸命、新潟をアピールしているところです。日本全国いいところはたくさんあるけれど、やっぱり新潟は「自分のふるさと」ですから。

最近は若い方に「ラスボス」なんて呼んでいただいて応援してもらって嬉しいです。この本のように若い人が新潟のために励んでいるのをみて、一緒に頑張りましょう！って思います。この地にいる人だから出来ることをね！

幸子さん、本当にありがとうございました！

小林幸子さん (70) | 歌手
1953年12月、新潟市横七番町生まれ。9歳まで新潟市で過ごす。現在は、新潟の農業を支援していく「幸せプロジェクト」や、新潟市観光大使など新潟を盛り上げようと精力的に活動を続けている。

取材・文　金澤李花子

Shopping

\ 買い物 るんるん♪ |

ヒメミズキで豊かな暮らしのヒントを得る

日本各地の作家さんの器を通して季節を感じ、文化に触れるお店「ヒメミズキ」。店主小笹教恵さんが各地から集めた器、柔らかな空気を纏った居心地の良い店内。センス良く生けられた花は店主の人柄を表すかのごとく空間に溶け込んで静かに佇む姿が気持ち良い。器目当てだけでなく、生活の知恵やたくさんのひらめきを与えてくれる小笹さんに惹かれて訪れる人も多い。何気ない会話の中に暮らしや心を豊かにするさまざまなヒントが在り、器と一緒に持ち帰ることができるヒメミズキは、器を扱うお店というだけでなく街や人、心や文化も育むかけがえのない場所だと思います。

HIMEMIZUKI: Tips for a Quality Lifestyle

Himemizuki, a charming tableware shop, curates exquisite pieces crafted by potters from across Japan. The owner, Ms. Kozasa, meticulously selects these items, resulting in a serene and soothing atmosphere within the shop. Tastefully arranged flowers reflect her personality and add to the comforting ambiance. Visitors are drawn not only to the tableware but also to Ms. Kozasa's wisdom and inspiring outlook on life. This shop is an indispensable haven for nurturing culture and enriching the mind.

高橋香織
初生雛鑑別師／加飾人（手仕事・ディレクション・器・フードスタイリスト）

Shopping

35

hickory03travelers
で新潟土産を探し出す

新潟のクリエイティブ集団がデザイン
した衣類や新潟土産、雑貨を制作、販売。
お勧め商品は新潟で120年以上続く、
あられが砂糖でコーティングされた伝
統菓子「浮き星」。飲み物、アイスクリー
ムにトッピングしても見た目が可愛い。
目移するほど種類があるおしゃれな缶
入り。木造2階建て築90年の酒屋を
活用した空間で買い物を楽しめる。「日
常を楽しもう」をコンセプトに地域に
根差した活動もしている。2階ギャラ
リースペースも必見。

HICKORY 03 TRAVELERS: Uncover Characteristic Niigata Souvenirs

This shop produces and sells clothing and
Niigata souvenir goods designed by a local
creative group. A standout recommendation
is the snack called "UKIHOSHI," rice crackers
coated in sugar. These star-shaped treats
make delightful toppings for ice cream or
drinks. The shop itself occupies a 90-year-old
building—a renovated old sake shop—making
it a fun place for shopping. Their motto?
"Enjoy daily life." And don't miss the second-
floor gallery—it's a must-see!

バセットみなみ
新潟生まれ、新潟育ち。イギリス夫と新潟の魅
力を再確認中、新潟を盛り上げたい。英語学童、
インバウンド旅行業。

36

上古町の百年長屋 SAN の浮き星

お花屋さん？カフェ？ロゴが書かれた看板は少しだけ曲がっている。中に入ると新潟のお菓子「浮き星」が並び、カウンターからは楽しそうな声が聞こえる。ここは上古町商店街の中にある小さな複合施設。お茶を飲んだり、おしゃべりしたり、勉強したり、過ごし方は人それぞれ。「何かをはじめてみたい、こんなことやってみたい」という人たちと、楽しくてちょっとヘンテコなイベントも開催。街に暮らす一人として、いつ来ても新しい刺激がある場所だ。

Sip on an Ice Cream Soda with Ukihoshi at HYAKUNEN NAGAYA SAN: A Perfect Treat for a Hot Day!

Florist? Cafe? The sign board is slightly tilted, but that adds to the charm of the place. When you enter, you're greeted with the sight of many pretty canned Niigata confectionaries called "ukihoshi" on display and you can hear cheerful voices from the counter. This is a small complex facility located in the Kami-Furumachi Mall. Everyone spends their time here in their own way, such as drinking tea, chatting, or studying. People who want to try something new or do something different hold fun and quirky events here. As someone who lives in this town, I always find new inspiration whenever I visit.

森千紘
上古町の百年長屋 SAN の喫茶の元スタッフ。現在は名古屋のデザイン事務所で働いています。

37

Atelier Cosette で フランスの小物に出会う

Atelier Cosette は、東堀通４番町にある青い壁が印象的なお店です。フランスで買付した小物、家具、服たちを優しい店主がその時の時代背景と共にご紹介してくれます。店内に入るとフランス旅行に来ているかのようなワクワクする気持ちを味わうことができます。蚤の市に行きたいけど県外行くのに躊躇っている人がいたらぜひこちらを訪ねてみてほしい。

ATELIER COSETTE: Curated Goods from France

On Higashibori Street's fourth block stands a shop with a striking blue wall. Step inside to discover carefully curated goods, furniture, and clothing—all sourced from France. As you browse, you might feel as though you've been transported to the charming flea markets of France itself.

茉奈
普段は新津で会社員をしています。古町は好きなお店がいっぱいあるので（主にコーヒー）よく通っています。

38

ノ縞屋で異国の雑貨に出会う

店主のセンスが光るトルコ、東欧、北欧などのアイテムが揃っているコンセプトストア。路地に佇む古くからの長屋を利用した店内はどこか懐かしく落ち着いた雰囲気で、木の温もりが北欧のシンプルなデザインにもマッチしています。「好きなものを集めたらこういう空間になった」と楽しそうに話してくれる店主。気取らずに接してくれる姿に長居をするお客さんも多いです。2023年で8周年を迎えて多くの方に訪れてほしいと語る店主に皆さんも一度会いにいってみては。

Explore Foreign Goods at NOSHIMAYA

At this concept store, the owner curates a delightful collection of selective items from Turkey, Eastern Europe, and Scandinavian countries. Housed in an old townhouse tucked away on a quiet street, the space exudes a nostalgic atmosphere. The wooden, simple Scandinavian-style design complements the setting. The owner joyfully shares, "gathering my favorite things led to the creation of this space." Visitors often find themselves lingering due to the friendly interactions with the owner. In 2023, the store celebrated its eighth anniversary, and the owner hopes to welcome even more visitors.

バセットみなみ

新潟生まれ、新潟育ち。イギリス夫と新潟の魅力を再確認中、新潟を盛り上げたい。英語学童、インバウンド旅行業。

39

ルルルで個性的な雑貨を探す

新潟市美術館のミュージアムショップはいつもたのしい。ときめくセレクトに店内の隅々まで練り歩いてニヤニヤ。ここで手に入れたものは私の生活に数知れず。美術館のショップというと展覧会グッズなイメージかもだけれど、ここでは併せて見て楽しい素敵なフェアもときどき開催しているのです。ルルルを会場に、多様な作家さんやお洋服ブランドなどの展示会。これって私はすごいと思う。もちろんショップだけの来館もお気軽に。なのでプレゼント探しにも足繁く利用しています。

Discover Unique Finds at LULULU, the Museum Shop at Niigata City Art Museum

LuLuLu, the museum shop at Niigata City Art Museum, is a treasure trove of unique and characteristic items. The shop's carefully curated selection never fails to excite me as I browse through it. My life is filled with items from this shop that I can't find anywhere else. LuLuLu is known for its special fairs featuring clothing brands and craft artists, making it the perfect place to find a one-of-a-kind gift for someone special. Everyone is welcome to come and explore this delightful shop!

近藤実可子

某刺繍のひと。作品展出品のほか、刺繍小物の製作販売、刺繍イラストでの挿絵や装丁など幅広く活動している。12年間育てていただきました、ありがとう古町大好きです。

40

APARTMENT でセンスの良い家具に囲まれる

素敵な家具、センスの良い雑貨に囲まれた心踊るゆったりとした空間。珍しくて cool な雑貨、温もりのある家具などに興味がある方は何度も訪れたくなる、そんな場所です。たまにふらっと立ち寄るとレイアウトが変わっていて新しい発見をすることができ、ワクワクでいっぱいです。そしてスタッフさんたちとの会話がとても楽しく、話し始めたら止まらなくなります。ぜひアパートメントに行ったらスタッフさんたちとお話ししてみてください。

APARTMENT: Elevate Your Lifestyle with Tasteful Life Goods and Furniture

This spacious store is filled with high-quality furniture and tasteful lifestyle goods that are sure to excite you. If you're someone who enjoys unique interior goods or furniture that create a comforting atmosphere, you'll want to visit this store repeatedly. You'll find that the shop's layout is frequently updated, leading to exciting new encounters with items. The staff is always friendly and engaging, making it fun to linger and chat with them. When you visit this store, be sure to take your time and enjoy the experience!

榎並詩乃
高校3年生で古町100選の広報を担当。もっと古町の魅力を色んな人に伝えていきたいと思っています。

Shopping

41

北書店で本を選ぶ至福の
ひとときを過ごす

萬代橋を渡って海のほうへやすらぎ堤
を歩くと見えるのはエスカイア大川前
プラザ。その一階にひっそりと佇むの
が2022年に市役所前から移転オープ
ンした北書店です。北書店は私が本を
好きになったきっかけでした。今の私
につながる大切な思い出がたくさん。
佐藤店長セレクトの本たちに、いつも
栄養を与えてもらっています！穏やか
でぬくもりのある店内でゆっくりと本
を選ぶ時間が至福のひととき。長く続
いてほしい本屋さんです。

KITASHOTEN: Find Your Next Book for Quality Time

Across the Bandai Bridge towards the Yasuragi-tei river bank you will find the Esquire Okawa-mae Plaza condominium. The first floor of this building houses the Kita Shoten bookstore, which was relocated in 2022. Kita Shoten is a bookstore that has made me fall in love with books. The manager, Mr. Sato, has a great selection of books that have nourished my mind. Choosing a book at their warm and serene store is a blissful experience. I hope this place continues to thrive for years to come.

宇野友恵｜RYUTist
古町を拠点に活動するアイドルグループ
RYUTist のメンバー。デビュー以来12年ほぼ
毎日古町に通ううちに、今では新潟のお店巡り
が趣味に。

萬松堂にふらりと立ち寄る

古町モール６にある、ザ・街の本屋さんという感じが心地よい、萬松堂。小さい頃、海外なんか行ったことなかったのに、まるでニューヨークにあるおしゃれなビルに入ったかのような高揚感があった。特に２階から吹き抜けを見下ろす感じが良い。待ち合わせ場所を萬松堂にしたら、少し早めにきてふらっと本を探すのがオススメ。

Visit BANSHO-DO, a Classic Bookstore in Furumachi

Bansho-do is a charming bookstore located on the 6th block of the Furumachi Mall. It's a cozy kind of place that's becoming increasingly rare in towns these days. As a child, I was always excited to visit this building, which reminded me of the bookstores in New York. One of the best things about Bansho-do is the view from the second floor, which is open to the lower level. If you're meeting someone at Bansho-do, be sure to arrive early so you can browse your favorite books.

TARO ｜ Bar Hallelujah

Bar Hallelujah 店主。クラフトジンと、冬はホットチャイラムがおすすめ。

コットンハウス 39 の
生地で洋服を作る

古町商店街６番町の細い通りにある生地屋さん。コットンやリネンなどの自然素材を中心に取り扱っていて、オーナーの金井さんの広い知識や雑学がとても面白い。私自身 18 年前の学生時代からずっと通い、布や糸、ボタンなど購入したり、金井さんの雑談を聴いたりしている。「買っては捨てる消費する衣服」という存在から、「ずっと持っていたい宝物のような衣服」に巡り逢いたいのなら、まずは 39 さんで針と糸とボタンを手に入れて、外れてしまったボタンを付け直してみるのはいかがでしょうか。

COTTON HOUSE 39: Timeless Textiles for Wonderful Expression

In the 6th block of Niigata's historic Furumachi district, there lies a textile haven. This unassuming shop, nestled on a small alley, offers an array of cotton, linen, and other natural materials. The proprietor, Kanai, possesses a wealth of knowledge and shares intriguing tidbits with patrons. Personally, I've frequented this store since my student days—purchasing fabrics, threads, and buttons while soaking in Kanai's captivating tales. If you lean toward cherishing durable garments over disposable ones, drop by for needles, thread, and buttons to mend that missing button on your shirt.

佐藤悠人｜ UTOPIA

古町の服飾専門学校卒業後、2017 年ブランド UTOPIA 起業。地場産業・伝統と共にテキスタイルから服を作る。

Shopping

UTOPIA の洋服で旅へ の思いを膨らませる

「旅する衣」がテーマのファッションブランド。とある 19 歳の主人公が旅をする中での体験や経験を通じて成長していくストーリーを衣服に落とし込んでいる、という素敵すぎるコンセプト。店主の悠人さんはとても気さくで優しく、悠人さんとお話ししながら、いろんな服試して、悩んで、その度にワクワクする。そして気が付いたら時間が経っていて、手にはひとつのアイテムが。いろんな場所へ旅をしたくなる、そんなお気に入りのアイテムに出会える場所です。

渡邊健吾
KENGO COFFEE ／和太鼓演奏者。古町にはどこか懐かしい雰囲気がありつつ、新しい出会いや発見がある場所。まだ知らない古町に出会えるのを楽しみにしています。

Discover clothes that inspire wanderlust at UTOPIA.

Utopia is a fashion brand that specializes in clothes that make you want to travel. The brand's concept is based on the story of a nineteen-year-old character who travels and grows up. Yuto, the designer, is a frank and kind person, so talking with him and trying on his garmets is always exciting. You will find your favorite item that will make you want to go to many places.

45

Rerun でフェアトレード
ファッションを知る

オーガニックコットンや手作り、伝統
技術を活かした洋服や小物を取り扱っ
ている。細かい手刺やデザインに目を
奪われるアイテムや、新潟の作家の商
品にも出会える店。フレンドリーな店
主の説明を聞くと、それぞれの商品の
ストーリーに引き込まれる。商品はど
れもていねいで、作り手の想いにあふ
れるものばかり。試着も気軽にできま
す。オーガニック食品も取り揃えてあ
り、可愛いデザインのチョコレートは
贈り物にも自分へのご褒美にも最適。

RERUN: Embrace "Fair-Trade" Fashion

Explore organic cotton items, handmade
clothes, and accessories that showcase
traditional techniques from various countries.
Delicate embroideries and thoughtful designs
catch your eye. Additionally, discover Niigata-
based creators' items. The friendly owner
provides insightful explanations about each
selected piece. Don't hesitate to try on these
carefully crafted fair-trade items. You'll also
find organic foods and charmingly packaged
chocolates—perfect as gifts or personal treats.

バセットみなみ

新潟生まれ、新潟育ち。イギリス夫と新潟の魅
力を再確認中、新潟を盛り上げたい。英語学童、
インバウンド旅行業。

46

ASYLUM で自分らしい
仕上がりを見つける

日和山神社という小さな神社のすぐ
下、路地の先にあるジブリのような庭
を構えた古い一軒家が古着屋 ASYLUM
です。店長が中古のお洋服を一枚一枚
チェックして、良質な「仕上がり」の
もののみを取り揃えています。素材、
デザイン、考え抜かれた服を着ること
が、自己表現につながり、その人らし
い「仕上がり」になるらしい。とても
思想的に話しましたが、要はお洒落で
一癖二癖あるお洋服がいっぱい揃って
います。日々にスパイスを与えてくれ
るお洋服たちばかりです。いつもとは
違う自分に出会えます。

ASYLUM: Find Your Style

Asylum is a used clothing store located just
at the bottom of Hiyoriyama shrine. The
shop is housed in an old house with a yard
that looks like it came straight out of one of
Studio Ghibli's films. The owner has carefully
curated a collection of high-quality garments
that are sure to impress. The clothes are well-
considered in terms of material and design,
which allows you to express yourself in unique
ways. In short, Asylum is home to many
fashionable one-of-a-kind items that will help
you spice up your wardrobe and discover a
new you.

吉田麻希

古町に映像制作会社の事務所を構え働いていま
す。私の衣食住は古町に支えてもらっています。

Shopping

古着ストリート（上古町）でファッションに出会う

Discover Unique Fashion at USED CLOTHES STREET in Kami-Furumachi: You never know what you might find!

古町通りには多くの古着屋さんがあり、その中でも一番小さくて、一番密に接客をしてくれる店をこっそり教えたい。1グループしか入れない店内だが、店主がお客の雰囲気や体型からしっくりとその人がよく見える服を提案してくれる。また、普段なら選ばないような服も提案してくれ、戸惑いながら試着するも、気に入って連れて帰ってしまう。そのワクワクをまた味わいたくて通ってしまう。どうしても滞在時間は長くなってしまうので、時間がある時にゆっくり服を選んでほしい。店名は言わないが、行けば分かるだろう。

Furumachi Street in Niigata is home to many used clothes stores. I'd like to tell you about a small and friendly shop in the area. Although it can only accommodate one group of customers at a time, the owner is very helpful and will suggest clothes that fit you well and suit your style. You might find something new and exciting to try on, and you'll probably end up buying it. The experience is so enjoyable that you'll want to come back again and again. Take your time and enjoy choosing your favorite clothes. I won't reveal the name of the shop, but I'm sure you'll find it eventually.

真保由樹

介護の仕事が少しでも良いイメージになればと思う介護士。休みの日を高確率で晴らす晴れ屋さん。学生の頃から古町に通い、常にお気に入りのお店を探し通っている。

![48]

shabby sic ポエトリーで新しい音楽を発見する

古町地区、東堀通の小さな路地に佇むレコードと CD、音楽にまつわるグッズを販売しているお店。j-pop からアングラヒップホップまで、店主の趣向を凝らし、セレクトされたレコード、CD がずらりと並びます。行くたびに知らなかった新しい音楽を発見できます。不定期に週に 1、2 日のオープンするお店です。詳細は X（旧 Twitter）にて発信されていますのでぜひチェックしてみてください！

ke-shiki
新潟市北区で木製オリジナル・オーダーの家具と美容室を営む施設を運営しています。古町は行くたびに新しいモノやコト、ヒトに出会える場所！

SHABBY SIC POETRY: Experience a New Genre of Music

Located on Higashi Bori Street in Furumachi, this music shop offers a wide range of records, CDs, and music-related goods. The owner's passion for music is evident in the carefully curated collection that includes genres ranging from J-pop to underground hip-hop. The store is known for its ever-changing inventory, so you can expect to discover new music every time you visit. Please note that the store opens randomly once or twice a week.

Shopping

57

SunBake のパンで最高の休日を始める

SunBake のパンは、味わいはもちろん、こだわりの素材を使用し、思わず手に取ってしまいたくなるサイズ感です。温かい接客で、オープンからたくさんのファンに愛されています。オーナーは東京でパンの修行後Uターン。やわらかい甘さとほのかに感じる酸味のバランスが最高のレーズンブレッドがおすすめ。朝は7:30からオープンしているので、休日も早起きして、SunBake のパンとコーヒーを買うと素敵な休日になること間違いなし。

渡邊健吾
KENGO COFFEE ／和太鼓演奏者。古町にはどこか懐かしい雰囲気がありつつ、新しい出会いや発見がある場所。まだ知らない古町に出会えるのを楽しみにしています。

SUNBAKE: Start Your Day Off Right with Delicious Bread and Coffee

Sun Bake's bread is made with quality ingredients and its size makes it irresistible. The bakery is known for its kind service and has many fans. The owner, who is originally from Niigata, has experience baking in Tokyo and has brought his expertise back to Niigata. We recommend trying their raisin bread, which is a customer favorite. Sun Bake opens at 7:30 am, so if you're an early riser, their bread and coffee are sure to make your day wonderful.

50

みなと街ベーカリーで
パンを買ってみなとぴあへ

早川堀通り沿いにあるパン屋さん。コッペパンの種類が豊富。定番のジャムパンや季節のフルーツを使ったものあります。オススメはあんバターコッペ。あんこの素朴な甘さ、バターのコッテリ感、歯切れよくモチモチしたコッペパンがマッチした最高の一品です。ハード系だとフルーツがぎっしり入ったカンバーニュもオススメ！みなとぴあはみなと街ベーカリーから徒歩7分くらいなので、水の流れる音や自然に囲まれて、ボーッとしながらパンを食べるのが最高。

MINATOMACHI BAKERY: A Must-Visit Destination for Bread Lovers

Located along Hayakawa-bori Street, Minatomachi Bakery is popular and offers a wide range of bread. Their sandwich bread with jam or seasonal fruits is a customer favorite. We recommend trying their sweet bean paste with butter sandwich or rich butter with simple bean paste. The chewy but crusty texture of their bread roll sandwich is worth a try. Additionally, their signature bread, Pain de Campagne, is a hard bread with densely mixed dried fruits. Pick up some bread and then enjoy it at Minatopia, which is located just seven minutes away on foot.

鈴木太朗

新潟市駅前のホテルに勤務。古町は独特の落ち着いた空気感があります。良いお店がたくさんあるので「もてなす」という空気感が広がった場所だと思っています。

Shopping

51

冨士屋で昔ながらの
クリームパンを買う

昔から古町に根付くパン屋「冨士屋」。全国の品評会で最優秀賞を受賞した角食パンが人気だが、個人的にはクリームパンも有名でおすすめ。「やっぱり美味しい！」と、安心の味。古町本店のほか、イトーヨーカドー内の店舗がありますが、展開するパンの種類は少し異なる様子で両方足を運びたいところ。

小林恵子
気が付くと古町を拠点に働いて２０年。父母も古町で働いた経験がある。もはや運命です。英会話インストラクターをしています。

FUJIYA: Nostalgic Custard Cream Buns Await You

Deeply rooted in Furumachi's history, Fujiya bakery boasts national-level award-winning sandwich bread. Personally, I recommend their comforting custard cream buns. With two locations—one on Furumachi and another at Ito Yokado on Honcho Street—both shops offer a delightful variety of bread and pastries.

52

luxuoso で魔法のような
コーヒー豆を買う

LUXUOSE: Your One-Stop Shop for Premium Coffee Beans

Luxuose is a specialty store that offers premium coffee beans to coffee lovers. While the barista-brewed coffee is the best, the store's beans enable anyone to make good coffee at home. Previously, coffee was served at the store, but now it specializes in the sale of coffee beans. If you have trouble making good coffee, visit Luxuose and you will magically be able to elevate your morning coffee experience.

東堀にあるコーヒー豆の販売専門店、ルシュオーゾ。コーヒーは本来バリスタに入れてもらうものが一番だが、ここのコーヒー豆は誰がどこで淹れても美味しい。昔はコーヒーを淹れることもしていたらしい。今はコーヒー豆の販売に特化している。コーヒーを淹れるのが苦手な人は、ここに足を運べば毎朝のコーヒーが楽しみになる魔法のようなお店。

TARO | Bar Hallelujah
Bar Hallelujah 店主。クラフトジンと、冬はホットチャイラムがおすすめ。

53

笠原豆店で店主の笑顔に癒される

いつも笑顔で元気いっぱいの笠原姉妹がいるお店。人情横丁の端っこにあります。大きな柿の種やピーナッツ、美味しい弥彦名物のカレー豆などを販売するほか、いろんなお菓子がかわいく並んでいます。店内の写真など楽しいですよ。僕はよく県外からの来訪者を連れていきます。なんと言っても笠原さんの笑顔に癒されます。騙されたと思って、ぜひ行ってみてください。商店街の豆まきに落花生などくださいます。ファンです。

Meet the Smiley Owners of KASAHARA BEAN SHOP

At the end of Ninjo Yokocho shopping mall in Niigata, you'll find the Kasahara sisters' shop. They are always smiling and welcoming to visitors. The shop offers a variety of snacks, including big-sized kakinotane peanuts and delicious yahikomame curry-flavored broad bean snacks. You can also find various other kinds of snacks laid out in the shop. The walls are adorned with many pictures, making it a fun place to visit. I often bring visitors to Niigata from other places, and they always leave with a smile on their face. I'm a big fan of the Kasahara sisters!

迫一成

hickory03travelers ／合同会社アレコレ代表／上古町の百年長屋 SAN 館長。イラストとデザインと社会とちょっと変わっているものとおだやかなものが好き。

54

さわ山でお土産に名代大ふくをまず選ぶ

大正時代から続く人気店で「大福と言えばここ！」というファンも多い。さわ山の大福の特徴は、餅の部分が薄くて、あんこの量が多いこと。ふわっとしている餅からこぼれ出る小豆感はたまりません。結構大きいのにいくつも食べられる気持ちになり危険。食べたことの無い方にはぜひ一度頑張ってほしい大福です。

SAWAYAMA: Sweet-Tooth Heaven with Daifuku-Mochi

Since the early Taisho era (1916-1926), Sawayama has captivated fans with its daifuku mochi. These delicate treats feature sweet bean paste enveloped in thin mochi. Each bite reveals a harmonious blend of robust and delicate sweetness—a dangerously delightful experience. Don't miss out on trying this exquisite daifuku!

小林恵子

気が付くと古町を拠点に働いて２０年。父母も古町で働いた経験がある。もはや運命です。英会話インストラクターをしています。

55

上野屋本店で柔らかいみたらし団子を食べる

上野屋本店さんは、礎町通りの餅菓子屋さん。季節の餅菓子やおむすびなどが朝から並んでいます。先日伺った時は三色団子が並んでいて、雪が降る中、季節ごとに変わる餅菓子に春の訪れを感じます。そんな三色団子に心を奪われつつ、結局買ってしまうのはどんな季節でも「みたらし団子」です。朝早くに伺うと出来立ての柔らか〜いみたらし団子もあります。お餅を包んでくれる包装紙の香りもとてもとても癒されます。やっぱり安心できるこの味に帰ってきてしまうのですね。

Try Unique Rice Cake Dumplings at UENOYA HONTEN

Uenoya Honten on Ishizue-cho street offers seasonal rice cake sweets and rice balls. The shop has pre-season sweets to announce the advent of the new season. There is a wide variety of attractive sweets, but the mitarashi dumpling is a real crowd pleaser. Freshly made mitarashi dumplings are available in the early morning.

天野千尋｜atori

クロスパル新潟のほど近く、樋口新聞舗さんのお向かいで「atori」というお弁当屋をしています。山羊座、Ｏ型。好きな食べ物はそうめんとシュークリーム。

56

やま路で出来立ての
笹団子を頬張る

笹団子のやま路は、みなとぴあの近く
にある笹団子のお店です。やま路の笹
団子は甘さを抑えた笹団子で、早めに
いかないと売り切れることも多いと聞
きます。笹団子は蒸して仕上げること
がほとんどですが、こちらの笹団子は
茹でてあるため、硬めな食感が特徴的。
少し大きめで食べ応えもあるので、お
腹が空いた時のおやつにもぴったりで
す。食べる時に茹で直すと柔らかくな
るそうですよ。

YAMAJI: Freshly Boiled Sasadango
Delicately Wrapped in Bamboo Leaves

Yamaji is conveniently located near Minato
Pier. Their sasadango (sweet rice dumplings
wrapped in bamboo leaves) are less sweet
than those found in other shops, and they tend
to sell out quickly - so arrive early! Unlike the
usual steamed sasadango, Yamaji's version
is boiled, resulting in a denser and heartier
texture. When you indulge in these treats,
consider reboiling them for an even more
enjoyable experience.

小林恵子

気が付くと古町を拠点に働いて２０年。父母も
古町で働いた経験がある。もはや運命です。英
会話インストラクターをしています。

Shopping

57

小森豆腐店で豆乳ソフトクリームを食す

仕事の合間のひとやすみにちょうど良い。豆乳ソフトクリームを頼み受け取ったら、テーブルセットに腰掛ける。店内でいただけるなんて、なんて親切なんだ。と思う。テレビがついていて、家では観ない昼のワイドショーを凝視しながら自分のペースで味わう。その間にも常連さんが入れ替わり立ち替わり、ご近所の生活ものぞく。ついでにおぼろ豆腐、がんもどき、厚揚げ、野菜豆腐、おから、気になって買いすぎてしまう、けどすぐに食べちゃうのは常だ。

近藤実可子
某刺繍のひと。作品展出品のほか、刺繍小物の製作販売、刺繍イラストでの挿絵や装丁など幅広く活動している。12年間育てていただきました、ありがとう古町大好きです。

Enjoy Soy Milk Soft Serve Ice Cream at KOMORI TOFU

Komori Tofu is an ideal spot to take a break from work and indulge in some delicious soy milk soft serve ice cream. The eat-in corner with a TV is a customer-friendly setting where you can watch random variety shows while enjoying your ice cream. You can also overhear regular customers' conversations. In addition to the soft serve, Komori Tofu offers a variety of tofu dishes such as oboro tofu, ganmodoki or fried tofu with vegetables, fried tofu, vegetable tofu, okara (soy pulp), and many more.

58

FKm（エフケーメゾン）で本格ジェラートを堪能

新潟の美味しいもの好きの人々のきっと拠り所であろう古町１０番町にある「喜ぐち」さん。そのお向かいで2020年に open したスティックパイとジェラートのお店です。あの「喜ぐち」さんが全力全身で営むお店はやっぱり美味しい尊敬するお店です。材料にこだわった色とりどりのメニューたちは２階のイートインスペースでもいただけます。夏場はそのまま古町散歩も。もちろん「喜ぐち」でも食べられます。シメのタンメンも魅力的ですが、ジェラートと日本酒も魅惑的で困ります。

Try authentic Gellato at FK MAISON.

FK Maison is a Niigata foodies' hangout area. It is a gelato and stick pie shop located on the 10th block of Furumachi. Quality ingredients are used to create various kinds of gellato. Eat-in on the shop's second floor or get it to go. It will be a great addition to your summertime Furumachi stroll. You can also go to Kiguchi, across the street, and enjoy the gelato as a dessert there.

豊島淳子｜BarBookBox

東中通にあるトールビル３階で Book Bar + Shop「BarBookBox STORE」を経営。古町８番町の洋酒バー カマラードが修行先。

地酒防衛軍 吉川酒店で
オススメの日本酒を聞く

店名のインパクトどおり地酒を愛する
店主が地酒を守るため活動している秘
密基地である。一本一本ていねいで細
かな説明を聞きながら新潟の酒を試飲
させていただいていると、自分も新潟
地酒の輪の中に入れてもらえたかのよ
うな至福の時間を楽しめる。個性的な
ラインナップのお酒も揃っていて、い
わゆる淡麗辛口の新潟のお酒とはまた
一味ちがうものも、オリジナルの瓶を
購入して少量から楽しめる。店主のオ
ススメがとにかく的確。接客も温かい。

**JIZAKE BOEIGUN YOSHIKAWA SAKE
SHOP: Choose Your Local Sake Defenders**

Jizake Boeigun Yoshikawa Sake Shop's
impactful name hints at its secret purpose:
it serves as the owner's base for protecting
local sake culture. At this shop, you can
sample a variety of sake while receiving
precise and informative lectures from the
owner. It's like becoming a part of Niigata's
rich sake world. The selection includes unique
kinds that diverge from Niigata's typical
"Tanrei-Karakuchi" (dry and clean) styles.
You can even purchase your own original
bottle or in small amounts. Expect accurate
recommendations and excellent service.

木村有希

教育系パラレルワーカー。元高校教師で地元新
潟の食と酒を愛して止まない人。幼少期の遊び
場は古町の雁木通り。

60

清水酒店で可愛いラベル のビールを買って散歩

まちの酒屋「清水酒店」さんにはクラ
フトビールと日本酒が冷蔵庫にひしめ
いています。風情がクールなやり手の
レコード屋さんのようで、個性的。さ
まざまなデザインの缶たちを見るのも
目に楽しく、清水さんにお酒の個性を
聞きながらじっくり選べます。その日
の気分でビールを選んで、そのまま海
の方角に散歩するもよし。心地よい季
節ならやすらぎ堤のどこか深呼吸する
もよし。

豊島淳子｜BarBookBox
東中通にあるトールビル 3 階で Book Bar +
Shop「BarBookBox STORE」を経営。古町
8 番町の洋酒バー カマラードが修行先。

**SHIMIZU LIQUOR SHOP: A Haven for
Craft Beer and Japanese Sake Enthusiasts**

Shimizu Liquor Shop is a treasure trove of craft
beer and Japanese sake. The shop boasts an
impressive collection of both beverages, which
are stored in the fridge. The shop's interior is
reminiscent of a cool record store, with various
beer or sake labels with cool designs that
are sure to catch your eye. The owner, Mr.
Shimizu, is knowledgeable about each item
and can provide inspiration for your beer or
sake selection.

Lunch + Dinner

出来立てが美味い！

青海ショッピングセンター
鈴木鮮魚店で昼飲み

場所は本町通六番町、アーケード街の中にある青海ショッピングセンター。鈴木鮮魚はその奥にある歴史ある鮮魚店。刺身定食や焼き魚定食、海鮮丼などご飯メニューもさまざまあるが、カップ酒や缶チューハイなどお酒メニューも充実しており、生ビールはプラカップで提供されるからといって侮ることなかれ、圧倒的回転による常に保たれている鮮度と美しいクリーミーな泡が最高。わたしはそのビールを飲みながら海老しんじょうや卵焼き、メニューにはないその日の揚げ魚や小鉢をたべる昼下がりが大好きです。

SUZUKI SENGYO: A Seafood Haven at Oumi Shopping Center in Honcho

The Suzuki Sengyo seafood shop is located at the Oomi Shopping center at the end of the Honcho 6th block. They offer a variety of seafood dishes such as a sashimi set, grilled fish set, and seafood bowl. You can also enjoy your meal with a refreshing drink such as sake or chuhai. In the afternoon, you can pair your beer with shrimp cake, egg roll, or the deep-fried fish of the day. Although draft beer is served in a plastic cup, it has a creamy foam top that never disappoints.

あこ｜mahorama

上大川前通６番町にて mahorama というカフェを 2023 年初めにオープン。明るいうちからお酒を飲むのが好きなので、昼飲みスポットとしての古町も啓蒙していきたい。

Lunch + Dinner

71

62

港すし 市場店で気軽に地物の寿司をつまむ

人情横丁にあるカウンター席だけのこぢんまりとした寿司店。四季を通して日本海の新鮮な魚介類が顔を揃えます。気軽に寿司をたしなむにはもってこいのお店。オススメはちらし寿司。お客さんの好みにあわせてネタをかえてくれたり、おまけしてくれたり！彩り豊かな一杯がいただける。職人さんとの会話を楽しみながら、おなかいっぱい、しあわせいっぱいの時間がここに。

MINATO SUSHI ICHIBATEN: Savor the Taste of Local Sushi

Minato Sushi Ichibaten is a small sushi bar located in Ninjo Yokocho. It is a perfect place to try sushi casually. The chef caters to the customer's preferences and sometimes even gives a bit extra! Chirashi sushi, which is sushi on a plate topped with sashimi, is recommended. You can enjoy your favorite chirashi sushi made with fresh seafood from the Sea of Japan, which is available throughout the year. Conversations with the chef are also fun and engaging. Happiness comes with sushi!

高橋紘子
古町に住んで 15 年。食べて、飲んで、癒されて、私の体は古町でできています。

63

藪蕎麦のそば前をつまみに昼からぐいっと一杯

藪蕎麦があるのは古町通 8 番町。飲み屋がひしめき合う夜の店エリア。その中でお昼時から周辺住民の方々で常に賑わっているのが藪蕎麦。日替わりのそばとご飯もののセットや季節ごとのお蕎麦（鴨南蛮そば、牡蠣そばなど）も魅力的だけれど、昼から瓶ビールや日本酒を飲みながら超充実のそば前をつくのも至福です。板わさ、たまごやき、自家製のさつま揚げ…。今日は蕎麦までたどり着けるかなあとコップをぐいっとするのがたまりません。

YABUSOBA: Day-drink at a Traditional Soba Restaurant

Yabusoba is a traditional soba restaurant located in the 8th block of Furumachi. The restaurant is popular among locals during lunch hour. Yabusoba offers a variety of dishes, including daily lunch sets and seasonal soba. In addition to these, the restaurant also serves bottled beer and Japanese sake, which pair perfectly with their traditional side dishes such as egg roll, and house-made fishcake. If you're looking for an authentic soba experience in Niigata, Yabusoba is definitely worth a visit.

あこ｜mahorama
上大川前通 6 番町にて mahorama というカフェを 2023 年にオープン。明るいうちからお酒を飲むのが好きなので、昼飲みスポットとしての古町も啓蒙していきたい。

Dr. 可児の不思議な日替わりランチで元気を出す

人の温かみを感じたくなった時にふと吸い込まれる、Dr. 可児さん。お昼時に座るとランチは（ほぼ）自動的に「その日のおまかせ」だ。マスターの広瀬さんがつくるご飯は、時々説明のつかないメニューもあるのだが、そのランダム感が心地良く楽しみで定期的にお邪魔している。考えてみれば、自分の食べたいものを選ぶという行為に慣れすぎているな。お昼ご飯だって、もっと自由でいいんだな。そう思わせてくれるカミフルの名店です。

DR. KANI: A Unique Lunch Experience

Dr. Kani is a restaurant that offers a unique lunch experience. When you miss the warmth of people, Dr. Kani is the perfect place to visit. Once you are seated, you will be served the daily lunch special automatically. The restaurant's chef, Mr. Hirose, is known for his unique and creative dishes that are beyond description. It's always a fun time at Dr. Kani. It's no wonder why I make my way to this restaurant from time to time. Lunch can be more free-style here, and that makes me feel so good.

金澤李花子
上古町の百年長屋 SAN 副館長、編集者。
妄想図「踊り場」をフリーペーパーにしたところから SAN のプロジェクトをスタート。

65

ベルビューで信濃川を
見ながら朝食をとる

なんだかモヤモヤするときは、とっておきの朝食にいきます。新潟グランドホテル フランス料理ベルビューは、やわらかな色調のインテリアが素敵なレストランです。ゆったり流れる信濃川を眺めながらつやつやふわふわのスクランブルエッグをいただくと自分を取り戻していけるような、とてもとてもおだやかな気持ちになります。宿泊していなくてもこだわりの新潟ブランド食材が一度に楽しめることも魅力です。疲れた時こそ、朝から嬉しい予定を入れたいものです。

Take in the Shinano River over Breakfast at BELL VIEW

Bell View is a nice restaurant with soft-colored decor that offers a special breakfast with a view of the slowly-flowing Shinano river. The fluffy scrambled eggs will make you happy, and you can enjoy local Niigata produce used for breakfast even without staying at the hotel. When you're tired, get a power breakfast here.

天野千尋｜atori
クロスパル新潟のほど近く、樋口新聞舗さんのお向かいで「atori」というお弁当屋をしています。山羊座、O型。好きな食べ物はそうめんとシュークリーム。

66

オーベルジュ古町で老舗
フレンチの味を楽しむ

いつか行こうと考えていて数年前にはじめて足を運びました。上古町にある老舗のフレンチレストランです。いつもゲストに寄り添ったやわらかで行き届いたサービスをしてくださる、ちょうどよい大きさのレストランが近所にある嬉しさは格別です。正統派からあたらしい息吹までともに感じられるお皿たちはいつも見事です。前もって予約して、りゅーとぴあでのコンサート帰りにオーベルジュさんで思う存分ゆっくり美味しい時間を過ごす機会をずっとあたためています。

Enjoy French Cuisine at AUBERGE FURUMACHI

Auberge Furumachi is a long-established restaurant in the upper Furumachi area that offers authentic French cuisine. The restaurant is known for its good service and beautiful dishes that are both authentic and innovative. My dream is to come here and enjoy some down-time after a concert at Ryutopia.

豊島淳子｜BarBookBox
東中通にあるトールビル3階でBook Bar＋Shop「BarBookBox STORE」を経営。古町8番町の洋酒バー カマラードが修行先。

スパイスプッシャー 164
のあいがけカレーを食す

西堀通り交差点にあるカラフルな外壁
のカレー屋さん。毎日ラインナップの
変わるカレーは、あいがけで3種類味
わうのがオススメ。一口食べるとスパ
イスの香り・旨みに酔いしれ、多幸感
に包まれる。さらに、カレー同士を混
ぜることで複雑な味わいも楽しむこと
も◎ 番号札代わりに渡される動物フィ
ギュアは、カレーが出来上がるまでの
待ち時間にわくわく感を与えてくれる
存在。「良い1日を〜」と送り出してく
れる店主の優しい声がけも嬉しい。

SPICE PUSHER 164: Indulge in Curry and Embrace a Sense of Euphoria

At an intersection on Nishibori street, you'll find a colorful-walled curry shop that offers a different choice of curry every day. You can choose two or three of them and have them together. A spoonful of curry will mesmerize you with its aroma of spice and umami, and make you feel euphoric. While waiting for your order, you will receive an amusing animal figure as your order number. The owner's kind voice wishing you a nice day will make you happy after all.

平松世梨亜

古町（しもまち）出身。東京から新潟へ拠点を
移し、まちに関する活動を行なっているクリエ
イティブディレクター。古町が大好き。

Lunch + Dinner

68

サンドネで小皿料理と
クラフトビールを楽しむ

新堀通に 2023 年 4 月にオープンした
ばかりの居酒屋。店長が自ら市場へ赴
き、自身が選び抜いた鮮魚や食材を自
由な発想で調理する小皿料理はどれも
逸品です。また、クラフトビールはタ
イミングによっては「樽生」で楽しむ
ことができます。店内は、木の温もり
とシックな雰囲気を感じられる落ち着
いた空間です。カウンター席で一人で
食事をするも良し、テーブル席で気の
置けない仲間と飲みかわすも良し、さ
まざまなシーンで気軽に訪れることが
できるお店です！

SANDONE: Unwind with free-minded tapas and craft beer

This Izakaya is located on Shibbori street
and opened its doors in April 2023. The
owner himself goes to the market to procure
fresh seafood and ingredients, which are
used to prepare excellent dishes. Craft beers
are available on tap at specific times. The
cozy wooden and chic interior creates a cool
atmosphere, and you can enjoy yourself at
the counter or with your pals at the table. This
place is perfect for any casual occasion.

永井大地
新潟南高校出身。株式会社モアソビ代表。
2022 年 12 月に「古町夜市」を開催。豪雪の
悪天候にも関わらず約 400 名の来場で盛り上
り、今後も継続して開催していく予定。

69

ZA'ATAR（ザータル）
で中東フレンチを楽しむ

古町 9 番町の路地である日ふと見つけ
たビストロには「ザータル」とありま
した。メニューには見慣れないレバノ
ンやイスラエルのワイン。カウンター
にはスパイスがずらり。ふと入ってか
らずっと、あそこで今日は何を食べよ
うと思い浮かべる信頼するお店のひと
つです。料理もワインも異なる個性の
美味しさのぶつかり合いがたのしいお
店です。しっかりとお腹を空かして、
貪欲に美味しいものたのしむことを欲
している人におすすめします。ワイン
はボトルでぜひ。

Middle eastern-style French food at ZA'ATAR

ZA'ATAR is a restaurant that offers Lebanese
and Israeli wine. The assortment of spices
on the counter is sure to catch your eye. The
chemistry of dishes and wine will appeal to
those who have an appetite for delicious food.
Also, you can enjoy wine by the bottle.

豊島淳子 ｜ BarBookBox
東中通にあるトールビル 3 階で Book Bar ＋
Shop「BarBookBox STORE」を経営。古町
8 番町の洋酒バー カマラードが修行先。

70

モルゲンロートでドイツ
ビールとソーセージ

古町にいながら、ドイツ気分を味わえ
るドイツビール専門のビアホール。店
内にはくるみ割り人形や（ドイツの？）
陽気な音楽が流れている。私がいつも
オーダーするのが「ドイツ樽生セッ
ト」。ビールと相性抜群なソーセージや
ジャーマンポテト、ドイツパン、ザワー
クラフトのプレートと樽生ビール２杯
もついているので、家族や友人とシェ
アして乾杯している。店主の無駄のな
い仕事ぶりも華麗で、素敵。

MORGENROT: Enjoy authentic German beer and sausages

Check out Morgenrot, a German beer
specialty restaurant in Furumachi. The
restaurant offers a cozy atmosphere with
nutcracker dolls and German music playing
in the background. My regular order is their
German tap beer set that comes with a
plate of good sausages, German potato,
sauerkraut, and two glasses of beer. It is plenty
enough for sharing with family and friends.
The owner's practical work is also impressive.

平松世梨亜
古町（しもまち）出身。東京から新潟へ拠点を
移し、まちに関する活動を行なっているクリエ
イティブディレクター。古町が大好き。

Lunch + Dinner

71

ピッツェリア・ダ・ヴィットーリアのピザで誕生日会をする

小学生の頃初めてヴィットーリアのピザを食べた時の、こんなに美味しいピザあるんだ！という感情は今でも覚えている。本当に美味しくて毎年のように自分の誕生日になると、テイクアウトしてお家で食べていた。ここのピザはナポリ風の窯焼きピザ。マルゲリータにはたっぷりとモッツァレラがかかっている。何と言っても、こぢんまりとした雰囲気、小麦の香りが良く、店員さんの愛想も良いのでぜひ一度、足を運んでみてほしい。

Celebrate your birthday with pizza of PIZZERIA DA VITTORIA

I still remember my first amazing pizza experience at Vittoria when I was an elementary school student. It was so good that I would ask for a take-away on every birthday of mine and enjoy it at home. The restaurant serves Naples-style pizza, which is baked in a stone oven. The Margherita pizza comes with plenty of mozzarella cheese and is a must-try. The restaurant has a compact yet cozy atmosphere with the aroma of wheat in the air, and the staff are approachable and welcoming.

榎並詩乃

高校3年生で古町100選の広報を担当。もっと古町の魅力を色んな人に伝えていきたいと思っています。

72

TETTO で気軽に
一人飲みをする

テットさんは女性でも気軽に一人飲み
ができる、居心地の良いイタリアンレ
ストランです。2015 年上古町でオー
プンし、以前の雰囲気を残しつつ、西
堀通（鍛治小路）の築 50 年の味のあ
るビルへ移転しました。その同じ建物
の４階にあるテットスタジオという場
所では、よもぎ蒸しやヨガレッスンも
開催されており、お腹だけではなく、
心も身体も満たしてくれる穴場スポッ
トです。

TETTO: Enjoy a cozy Italian dining experience

TETTO is a cozy Italian restaurant located in the upper Furumachi area of Niigata. It offers a warm and inviting atmosphere to both solo diners and groups. Opened in 2015, the restaurant recently moved to a fifty-year-old building on Nishibori Street (Kaji-koji). On the fourth floor of this building, you can also find yoga classes and Korean-style Yomogi-mushi therapy. TETTO is not just about satisfying your taste buds, but also about nourishing your mind and body.

真下恵

元ノイズムダンサー。新潟市内を中心にヨガや
バレエ、コンテンポラリーダンスのレッスンを
開催。新潟に住み始めて約 16 年、古町に身も
心も捧げております。

レガロで個性的なネーミングからパスタを頼む

Order a Uniquely Named Pasta Dish at REGALO

Regalo is an Italian restaurant located on Furumachi sixth block. They offer various kinds of pasta dishes that are both delicious and filling. I usually stick to my favorite pasta, but they have other attractively named pasta dishes that you can't get enough of. It's a great place to visit time and again!

古町６番町にあるイタリア料理店、レガロ。さまざまな種類のパスタに目移りしてしまいます。味もボリュームも毎回満足しています。パスタを食べる時は個人的に冒険をせずに同じ物を食べる事が多いのですが、レガロはメニューにある名前からして惹かれるものがあり、そして意を決して頼んでも裏切らない味とボリューム。毎回行くのが楽しみなお店です。

miki ｜ Atelier Cosette
Atelier Cosette 店主。東堀通り４番町にあります、青い壁のお店です。フランスで買い付けた古い物達を取り扱っています。

リストランテ Sasaki で
豊富なメニューに目移り

友人と共に、魅力的な美味しいものワードが並ぶメニューをきらきらと眺める。ある時プッタネスカが目にとまり、無知だった私は名前が気になっただけでオーダーしてみた。それはトマトソースとオリーブのパスタで、美味しくて好きすぎて sasaki さんの虜になった。ピザもよく頼む。食事でお腹は満たされても、黒板にあるお初にお目にかかるデザートメニューが気になる。これもまたいつも私たちの想像を超えてくるのです。何をいただいても美味しいとうわさです。

SASAKI RESTAURANT: A Delightful Culinary Experience

Sasaki Restaurant offers a wide variety of dishes that are sure to satisfy your taste buds. Their puttanesca, a tomato pasta with olives, is a must-try and has been a personal favorite of mine. The pizza is also a crowd-pleaser. The desserts on the blackboard are hard to resist and are beyond imagination. Everything on the menu is delicious, which is why people can't stop talking about this restaurant.

近藤実可子

某刺繍のひと。作品展出品のほか、刺繍小物の製作販売、刺繍イラストでの挿絵や装丁など幅広く活動している。12年間育てていただきました、ありがとう古町大好きです。

Lunch + Dinner

広東で異国情緒あるチャイニーズレストランの雰囲気を味わう

ニューヨークにありそうなお洒落なお店で本格的な中華を食べられる中華料理屋、広東。冗談抜きにどれを食べても美味しい。エビチリは大きいエビと小さいエビの2種類から選べ、大きいエビのエビチリはかなりの食べ応えあり。紹興酒も充実していて、豊富なメニューから楽しめる。本格的な中華が楽しめるランチもあります。

KANTON: A Stylish Chinese Restaurant with Authentic NY Vibes

Kanton is a stylish Chinese restaurant that offers an authentic New York experience. The restaurant serves excellent Chinese food that is sure to delight your taste buds. Everything on the menu is delicious, and the chili prawns and shrimps are definitely worth a try. Kanton also boasts a great selection of shokoshu or Chinese Shaoxing rice wine. If you're looking for an authentic Chinese lunch, Kanton has got you covered as well. Come and experience the authentic Chinese food at Kanton!

TARO | Bar Hallelujah

Bar Hallelujah 店主。クラフトジンと、冬はホットチャイラムがおすすめ。

76

慶龍飯店のニンニクたっぷり餃子で週を締め括る

古町９番町にある、餃子が有名なカウンター席のみ老舗中華料理屋。愛想のいいご夫婦２人で切り盛りされています。壁には歴代の古町芸妓さんたちの千社札が貼られていてお座敷終わりの憩いの場にもなっているようです。一口放り込むと、強烈なニンニクが口から鼻にかけて広がりなんともビールが進む進む。無意識に２枚目を注文してしまうほど病みつきになる味です。次の日に人と会う予定がない週末にだけ食べられる特別なご褒美のようなお店です。あと細麺の焼きそばもおすすめ。

**Get Garlicky Chinese dumplings at
KEIRYU HANTEN**

Keiryu Hanten is a well-known Chinese restaurant located on the 9th block of Furumachi. The restaurant has a cozy counter and is run by a friendly couple. It is famous for its garlicky Chinese dumplings, which are really flavorful and go perfectly with beer. You might find yourself ordering a second serving without even realizing it! The restaurant is occasionally visited by Furumachi geisha after their work. If you're looking for something other than dumplings, we recommend trying their fried noodles.

今井雄介

古町生まれ古町育ち。普段はとある企業を経営しています。事業活動を通じて新潟の発展に微力ながら貢献出来ればと思います。

Lunch + Dinner

77

しののめへ仕事帰りに
立ち寄る

小路を入ると佇む、古民家をリノベーションした居酒屋。隠れ家的な存在で、何とも落ち着く空気感。仕事終わりに立ち寄り、カウンターですだちサワーをいただく。愉快な店主さんたちのおかげで笑いに癒やされ、疲れを忘れ、まさに良いデトックススポット。県内外の厳選された日本酒や新鮮な旬野菜もいただけるお店。その日に仕入れた新鮮なお野菜から作る「野菜酎ハイ」は美味しすぎて欠かしたことはない。ノンルコールでもいただけることができるので、野菜不足の方には特におすすめ。

Make a Pit Stop at SHINONOME on Your Way Home

Nestled in a small alley, Shinonome is a renovated traditional Japanese house izakaya that welcomes you with a cozy atmosphere. Drop by after work and enjoy a sudachi sour (soda and shochu with citrus fruit) at the counter. Interacting with the fun staff eases me from my busy day, which is so-called detoxing. Don't forget to order their tasty vegetable chuhai!

伊藤知香
普段は訪問看護師をしています。趣味でカメラを少々。古町に住んでいたこともあり、住み慣れたこの街並みが好きです。

写楽の夜定食を
食べながら店主と語らう

名前も含め、どうみても定食屋に見えない店構えの「写楽」さん。お店も2階にあるため、ふらっと入るのには勇気がいります。しかし、入ってみればカウンター席と小上がり席がある落ち着く空間。小鉢も充実している定食メニューが豊富。入店すると優しい店主のおばちゃんが「今日は仕事終わり?」なんて話しかけてくれる安心感。実家に帰ったような居心地の良さがあるため、転勤者が多い古町勤めの会社員もよく訪れているみたい。

A Warm Welcome Awaits You at
SHARAKU

Sharaku is a cozy but hard-to-find restaurant located on the second floor down a narrow alley. It offers a set menu with small side dishes. The tatami area and counter seats provide a comfortable and intimate atmosphere. The friendly owner will make you feel right at home, as if you were back at your parents' house. It's a great place to have a friendly conversation over dinner.

稲葉一樹

古町エリアに住まい、働いている公務員。かっこいい人がたくさんいる古町をもっと知ってもらい、どんどんそういう人が集まるエリアになってほしく微力ながら活動しています。

Lunch + Dinner

79

喜ぐちで新潟の郷土料理と酒にほっこりする

喜ぐちは古町通り10番町にある1965年創業の老舗の居酒屋です。お店の名前の由来は「お客さんの口を喜ばそう」から来ているそうです。新潟の地酒や郷土料理を思う存分楽しむことができます。先ずは餃子を食べ、お店のお母さんとしゃべって見たり、キョロキョロして誰か芸能人は居ないかと確認する。とにかく有名人がたくさん来ているお店です。

KIGUCHI: Comfort Food and Sake from Niigata

Nestled in Furumachi's tenth block, Kiguchi is a well-established izakaya. Its name, derived from "to delight the palate," perfectly suits their delectable offerings. Begin your culinary journey with their Chinese dumplings, engage in conversation with the friendly owner, and keep an eye out for any celebrity sightings.

稲垣青 | Blue Cafe

並木道にあるブックカフェ Blue Cafe のマスター。お店は古町で12年以上。スパイスカレーにこだわりあり。

さい三郎で名酒の村裕を飲み比べる

古町通り 11 番町にある、知る人ぞ知る老舗居酒屋。昔ながらの味のある佇まいに一歩入れば、新潟の地酒と、季節の地物食材を活かしたメニューがズラリと並ぶ。村祐はすこし「しゅわ」感があるお酒だが、何種類も置いているお店はとても珍しく、さい三郎ならではの楽しみだ。新潟の味覚を堪能できる店。

SAIZABURO: Appreciating Niigata's Famous Murayu Sake

Located on Furumachi's eleventh block, this lesser-known yet cherished izakaya awaits you. Step inside to discover an array of local sakes and seasonal dishes. The effervescent Murayu is a rare find on their menu, allowing you to savor its distinct flavors while soaking in Niigata's culinary delights.

小林恵子
気が付くと古町を拠点に働いて２０年。父母も古町で働いた経験がある。もはや運命です。英会話インストラクターをしています。

Lunch + Dinner

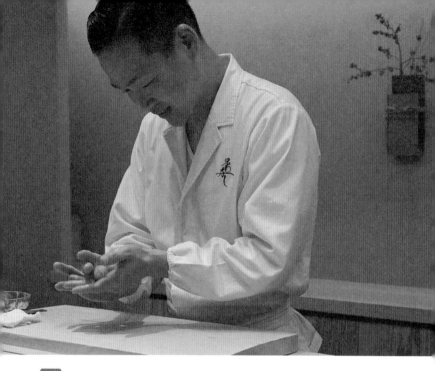

兄弟寿しの地物を使った
ていねいな江戸前寿司

鍋茶屋通にある兄弟寿し。新潟近海で
獲れた魚と新潟県産食材に、二代目店
主本間龍史さんのていねいな仕事×江
戸前鮨の技が施され、完璧な食べ頃で
提供される一品一品。ひと手間の極み
に出会える場所です。美味しさのあま
り食べ進める程に空腹感が増すような
感覚に陥るほど。店主の美しい手仕事
を見られるのも楽しみのひとつです。
店内は先代の頃から使用されていた備
品がところどころで使われるなど、歴
史を感じさせる内装も魅力です。

KYODAI SUSHI: Exquisite Edo-Mae Style Sushi with Niigata's Local Catch

Kyodai Sushi is a hidden gem nestled in the
9th block of Niigata's Furumachi district.
The alleyway entrance leads to one of the
city's finest sushi bars. Here, the owner, Mr.
Honma II, meticulously prepares sushi using
locally caught fish and Niigata's specialty
ingredients. The delicate craftsmanship and
Edo-style skills result in a culinary experience
that tantalizes the taste buds. As you dine,
you can be pleased by observing the chef's
graceful movements behind the counter in the
attractive interior equipped with items passed
down from the previous generation.

高橋香織
初生雛鑑別師／加飾人（手仕事・ディレクショ
ン・器・フードスタイリスト）

すゞ家の二階で秘密の作戦会議を行う

古町の超名店「すゞ家」さんには、県外客が来ると必ず連れていきたい。実は２階があるのはご存知だろうか？昔ながらの一室が残されているかのような空間で酒を酌み交わしていると、幕末の志士になったかのようなワクワク感を味わえる。地域を驚かせる企画や人に言えないくだらない話もここなら新潟の美味しい食事とともに、リラックスして語り合える。

SUZUYA: A Traditional Japanese Restaurant with a Private Guest Room

If you're looking for a unique dining experience in Niigata, Suzuya is the perfect place to take your guests. This famous restaurant offers a private guest room on the second floor, which is designed in a traditional Japanese style. The room provides an intimate setting where you can relax and enjoy Niigata cuisine while sipping sake here with your pals. It will make you feel like a Samurai. So, why not make a reservation at Suzuya and experience the best of Japanese hospitality?

稲葉一樹

古町エリアに住まい、働いている公務員。かっこいい人がたくさんいる古町をもっと知ってもらい、どんどんそういう人が集まるエリアになってほしく微力ながら活動しています。

鳥の歌で"お任せ"を
オーダーをする

栄養あるご飯が食べたい！となれば「鳥
の歌」に行って"お任せ"をオーダーし
ます。というか"お任せ"しかオーダー
したことありません。栄養バランスに
配慮したボリュームたっぷり美味しい
ご飯がお腹いっぱい食べられます。店
内には近々開催される公演チラシがた
くさん置いてあり、それらを見ている
だけでもとても楽しむことができます。

Nutritious Meal at TORINOUTA: Try the Chef's Special

If you're looking for a healthy and satisfying meal, head over to Torinouta! The chef's special is a great option if you're not sure what to order. You'll be served a voluminous and well-balanced meal that's sure to satisfy your hunger. While you're there, be sure to check out their assortment of flyers for more information about the town.

池ヶ谷奏
コンテンポラリーダンサー兼ダンス講師として
新潟と東京の2拠点で活動中。新潟に来た12
年前から古町近辺に住んでおり、新しくなって
いく店々と変わらない景色を楽しんでいる。

割烹やひこで晩酌セット
をオーダーする

独りでも大勢でも、どちらも良い。気
楽で落ち着いて、ていねいなお店です。
店の入口は二つ。居酒屋風の気楽な入
口と少し特別な入口。どちらから入る
か、迷ったものです。よく頼むのは、
晩酌セットと南蛮海老フライ。晩酌セッ
トは、刺身はもちろん、日によって異
なる肴の数点盛りが良い。南蛮海老フ
ライは、味もビジュアルも良い。酒と
会話が進みます。関東の知人のため、
自ら古町芸妓さんの会を催しました。
人生で初めてのこと。にぎやかな会と
なりうれしく、店主にも感謝。皆さん
も古町芸妓さんの会、ぜひ、やひこさ
んにて。

KAPPO YAHIKO: Order the Nightcap Set

Kappo Yahiko is a great place to come alone or with a group. The atmosphere is casual yet quiet, and the service is attentive. There are two entrances to the restaurant: one is a casual izakaya-style entrance, while the other is more special. My regular order is the Banshaku set and deep-fried Nanbamebi shrimp. The Banshaku set comes with sashimi or daily assorted appetizers to amuse your taste buds. The Nanbamebi shrimp fries taste as good as they look, and they're perfect for enjoying with sake and good conversation. I recently organized a party here with Furumachi Geigi (Geisha) for my acquaintances who came from the Tokyo area. It was my first experience, but the party was very fun, and I was thankful to the owner of this restaurant. I highly recommend having a party with Furumachi Geigi at Kappo Yahiko.

渡邉秀太
新潟市出身、市役所勤務。古町で8BANリノベー
ションなど、食・まち・地域・学びの切り口で
活動。古町は良い建物もあって、遺産を活かし
た飲み屋さんも大好き。

85

金辰で古町芸妓を呼んで女子会をする

一見さん大歓迎の古町花街は、お友達との飲み会や女子会にもおすすめです。金辰は昭和15年創業で歴史ある料亭の佇まい。とってもやさしい女将が出迎えてくれます。美味しい料理を楽しみながら古町芸妓さんの到着までそわそわ。芸妓さんは皆さんきさくで、お話し上手、そして個性豊か。踊りを鑑賞し、場が温まったらお座敷遊びタイム！古町の定番は「樽拳（たるけん）」。芸妓さんのかわいらしい掛け声と樽砧（たるきぬた）の心地よい音に合わせてじゃんけんぽん〜。お酒が入っていてもいなくても大盛り上がり。こうして花街の夜はあっという間に更けていきます。

KANETATSU: Host a party with friends and Furumachi Geigi (Geisha)

Furumachi Kagai is a vibrant nightlife district in Niigata, Japan. It is a perfect place for parties with friends, and welcomes first-time visitors with open arms. The district is home to many restaurants and bars, including Kanetatsu. Come and experience the charm of Furumachi Kagai!

はるにゃん

古町界隈育ちで、平日も休日も自転車で古町を駆け抜けているOL。社会人1年目に古町芸妓さんに出会い、今ではすっかりメロメロに。同年代のお座敷仲間を増やしたい。

Lunch + Dinner

古町を照らした
赤いネオンサイン

~新潟三越の記憶~

photographed
on Feb. 2001

　朝のまどろみの中でときどき見る夢がある。西堀通りを車で赤いネオンサインめざして買い物に向かう、新潟三越の夢。

　駐車場口から店内へ一歩入った瞬間の、ふわっと包み込んでくれるあのやわらかくて暖かな焼きたてのパンの香り。地階へ続くエスカレーターをまもなく通り過ぎると、パウダリーな空気が漂う化粧品フロア。美容部員さんのタッチアップにときめく人の横顔を通りしなに眺めながら、突き当たりのエレベーターを待つ。ホールのスピーカーからは店内放送が聴こえてくる。日中に10分刻みで流れてくる店内アナウンスは、やさしく落ち着いたトーンの中に華やかなきらめきを感じさせる、私が幼い頃からずっと変わらないいつもの声。

　「キンコーン」。シャンパンシルバーの扉がふっと開くも、このあたりで大抵夢は覚めてしまう。できればこの続きをあともう少しだけ見てみたいと願う。

　エレベーターの行き先は何階だろうか。お目当ての催し物に心ひかれて、まっすぐ7階にたどり着くのであろうか。それならば京都や北海道の物産展が開催されていたら、なおたまらない。できればそこには、ときおり空調の流れに乗って金寿や瓢亭の芳しい空気がふっと漂ってきてほしい。

　そして、あともう少し夢が続いてくれるならば、大食堂のファミリアでクリームソーダでも楽しみながら祖母といろんな話がしたかった。ガラス張りの席からはどんな古町が見えてくるだろうか。

　帰りはケーファーの惣菜に、ハロッズで紅茶も買って帰ろう。

　夕暮れ空に赤いネオンサインが昇る。新津屋小路のビルの谷間から顔をのぞかせては、家路に向かう私を最後まで見送ってくれる。

石田博道
新潟三越を長らく愛した新潟出身のグラフィックデザイナー。幼少期から30年以上にわたり新潟三越および周辺の街並みを見続けてきた。

Visit

お出かけ ランラン！

砂丘館で新潟の文化や暮らしを知る

新潟島の名所の一つ、どっぺり坂を登ったところにある、旧日本銀行新潟支店の支店長役宅の建物。季節を感じられるお庭とていねいにケアされ維持されている木造の立派なお宅で、なんだかゆったりした気持ちとすっきりした気持ちになれます。玄関を入ってすぐの洋間はとても良い感じ。贅沢空間の喫茶もとてもおすすめ。和室でこっそり横になったり、細い廊下をすたすた歩くのも楽しいです。奥の蔵などでは文化行事やダンス、展覧会や演奏などの催しもあり、文化や日本の暮らしを知れる最高の場所。

Explore Niigata's Culture and Life at SAKYUKAN

On top of the Dopperi-Zaka slope in Niigata, you'll find the former Bank of Japan Niigata Branch Manager's Residence, which is a popular sightseeing spot. The Japanese-style residence and garden are meticulously maintained and feature seasonal plants that create a calm and serene atmosphere. Upon entering the residence, you'll find a lovely Western-style room where you can enjoy tea time. You're free to walk around the house, lie down in the traditional Japanese room, and stroll through the corridors as if you were at home. The storage room on the premises is used for cultural events, dance performances, exhibitions, and musical performances.

迫一成

hickory03travelers ／合同会社アレコレ代表／上古町の百年長屋 SAN 館長。イラストとデザインと社会とちょっと変わっているものとおだやかなものが好き。

旧齋藤家別邸で
四季の移ろいを感じる

周りには老舗料亭「行形亭」や明治から昭和初期に建てられた建築物が多く残っています。ここだけ時間が止まったような雰囲気があり、喫茶もあるので、春夏は新緑、秋は紅葉に冬は雪（中央区はそんなに降らないけど…）など綺麗な庭園をみながらお抹茶と季節感あふれる和菓子（和生）を楽しめます。もともとは豪商・齋藤家がお客様をもてなすために建てたのがこの別邸だそうです。招かれたお客さま気分を味わえるのが醍醐味です。少し優越感にひたれますね。

THE SAITO VILLA: A Timeless Experience of Japan's Four Seasons

Saito Villa is a former summer estate originally owned by the successful shipping merchant, the Saito family, and used to entertain their guests. It is surrounded by historic ryotei, which are Japanese style high-end restaurants, including Ikinariya, and other splendid buildings that are over 100 years old. The atmosphere in this area is frozen in time. You can enjoy a view of the spectacular gardens that change with the season and appreciate Japanese-style tea and sweets in the tea room.

鈴木太朗
新潟市駅前のホテルに勤務。古町は独特の落ち着いた空気感があります。良いお店がたくさんあるので「もてなす」という空気感が広がった場所だと思っています。

Visit

88

県政記念館の周辺で
モダニズム建築を巡る

県政記念館、新潟市体育館、県民会館、音楽文化会館、りゅーとぴあ。ここは、さまざまな名建築が集まっているエリアです。集まっているが故にひとつひとつをじっくり見る機会が少ないのかもしれませんが、よくみると細部までこだわった建築物だということに驚かされると思います。どの建物も共通して窓の形が特徴的なのでぜひ窓に注目して見てほしいです。

NIIGATA PREFECTURAL GOVERNMENT MEMORIAL HALL: A Tour of Modernist Architecture

Niigata Prefectural Government Memorial Hall is one of several architectural masterpieces located in the area. Others include the Niigata City Gymnasium, Niigata City Music and Cultural Hall, and Ryutopia Niigata City Performing Art Center. These buildings are meticulously designed and feature unique window designs.

小笹教恵｜ヒメミズキ
古町通にて新潟県内外からセレクトした作家ものを取り扱う、うつわギャラリー「ヒメミズキ」を営んでおります。海から吹く風で季節をはっきりと感じ取れる新潟古町が好きです。

89

寄居諏訪神社で
心を落ち着かせる

新潟市中央区旭町にある寄居諏訪神社さん。新潟の街の中にぽっかりと現れる鎮守の森。静かで心落ち着く神社です。地域の人々からは親しみを込めて「おすわさま」と呼ばれています。人生開拓のご神徳があるとのことで、なにか頑張りたいことがある時にはおすわさまへお参りへ。そして、おかげさまで頑張れました、とお礼参りも忘れずに。敷地内には福をもたらすお稲荷さん「福一稲荷大明神」も。行事や季節ごとの御朱印も頒布されていますので、ご朱印帳を持って定期的にお参りするのもいいですね。

YORII SUWA SHRINE: Find peace of mind

Yorii Suwa Shrine is located in Asahimachi near the Niigata University hospital. The shrine is nestled in a small wooded area in the heart of the city, providing a serene and peaceful atmosphere. Locals affectionately refer to it as "Osuwa-sama". Some believe that the shrine offers benefits for cultivating one's life, so people visit it during life-changing events to pray. It is customary to return to the shrine after achieving success. Inari Shrine is on the same premises. This shrine is known for bringing good luck and offers special goshuin stamps for visitors during seasonal events. Regular worship with a stampbook can be an enjoyable experience.

小林あかね｜tricollage
手織り絨毯のデザイナー。東中通に tricollage（トリコラージュ）という絨毯店を運営。古町は青春時代を過ごした街。若い人たちの感性を磨けるような街であるといいな！

弘願寺の巨大な弘法大師にあたふたする

古町の繁華街を歩いていると突如、目を奪われる巨大な弘法大師像。新潟に住んでいると見慣れてしまって、その存在を見過ごしてしまうが、初めて見た時のインパクトは今でも忘れられない。まるで、特撮の世界に迷い込んだような気分になれる。調べてみたところ、このお寺が建立される前は、ここにストリップ劇場があったそうで、つわものどもが夢の跡を鎮めているかのよう。

KOGANJI TEMPLE: Encounter the Enormous Statue of Kobodaishi

In the heart of Furumachi's downtown area stands Kobotaishi statue, an unexpected sight that catches your eye. While Niigata locals may take it for granted, first-time visitors find it impactful. The temple's former life as a striptease theater adds an intriguing layer of history. Perhaps it now serves as a sanctuary for spirits who once reveled within its walls.

近藤潤

古町100選の主催者。デザイン＆一級建築士事務所 Suikaka 代表。高校の時、白寿のうま煮ラーメンのファンに。

Visit

91

旧新潟税関庁舎で
湊町新潟の情緒に触れる

湊町新潟を象徴する建物。度々の改修を重ねながら 150 年以上も前の建物を大切に守ってきた新潟市を勝手に誇らしく感じています。一見すると洋風の建物ですが、多くが和風の技術で造られているそうです。西洋建築の見よう見まね造った地元の大工さんの技術、尊敬します。歴史博物館にある明治時代の地図をみると当時の様子が少しわかりより楽しめると思います。

小笹教恵｜ヒメミズキ
古町通にて新潟県内外からセレクトした作家ものを取り扱う、うつわギャラリー「ヒメミズキ」を営んでおります。海から吹く風で季節をはっきりと感じ取れる新潟古町が好きです。

OLD NIIGATA CUSTOM BUILDING: A Symbol of Port Town Niigata

This over 150-year-old building is a symbol of Port Town Niigata. I am proud of Niigata city for carefully preserving it after several restorations. Although it looks like a western-style building, most parts are said to have been built using Japanese techniques. Carpenters tried to realize a western-style building while still respecting their traditional Japanese building skills. You can get an idea of life in the Meiji era (1800s) by looking at old maps displayed in the historical museum.

92

新潟絵屋で暮らしの中に
アートを感じる

下町風情そよがせる和風建築のギャラリー。この地域で一番新しい柳都大橋が開通した頃に、大正時代の町屋を今の場所まで移築したそう。企画展では絵画、彫刻、写真、工芸までさまざまですが、毎回ていねいに作家さんを選んでいて、ふと思い出した時に立ち寄ると、生活や思考に良い変化や気づきを与えてくれます。奥の部屋にフライヤーを置くスペースが広く取られていて、市内のアート系情報を収集するのにも最適です。

NIIGATA EYA : Feel art in your life

A traditional Japanese style house, this gallery stands as a testament to old-world elegance. Originally constructed during the Taisho era, this historic house was relocated when the Ryuto O-hashi bridge was built. Its carefully curated exhibitions span a rich tapestry of creativity, featuring paintings, sculptures, photographs, and crafts. Each display invites contemplation, sparking awareness and inspiring all who step through its doors. For the Niigata art enthusiasts, a treasure trove of art-related event flyers awaits, promising a journey into the vibrant world of creativity.

近藤潤
古町100選の主催者。デザイン&一級建築士事務所 Suikaka 代表。高校の時、白寿のうま煮ラーメンのファンに。

93

新潟市美術館で美術鑑賞をする

1985年に、隣接する西大畑公園とともにつくられた新潟市美術館。建築は、前川國男。最晩年を飾る作品として、建築関係の研究者や学生も見学に訪れる。閑静なエリアに作られ、美術鑑賞後には広々とした西大畑公園で一息つきながら、印象的だった美術作品への想いにふける。デジタルが発展する時代だからこそ、こうしたアナログな時間の価値をより感じとることができる場所です。

NIIGATA CITY ART MUSEUM: A Quiet Haven for Art Lovers

Designed by Maekawa Kunio in his latter years, the Niigata City Art Museum was built in 1985 near Nishi Ohata Park. Many architectural academics or students visit to appreciate its design. Located in a quiet area, you can reflect on your art experience while taking a break at the nearby park.

本間亘 | THE COFFEE TABLE

上大川前通で THE COFFEE TABLE というカフェを運営。海と川に囲まれた素晴らしいロケーションが古町の特長の一つだと思っています。

94

医学町ビル 2F ギャラリーで
新潟の現代アートや工芸に触れる

個性的な店が集まり、アートに触れられる空間。古風な佇まいのビルが、クリエイティブな活動の場に活用される。遊びとおもちゃの専門店、建築設計室、デザイン事務所、撮影スタジオなどが集まるほか、2 階の一室は貸しスペースとなっていて、陶器や雑貨・アート作品などの展示が開催される。趣のある部屋はギャラリーを開くにはうってつけの空間で、展覧会をしてみたい人にもおすすめ。勇気を出して入ってみてほしい。催しがある日の夕方は、貸しスペースに明かりが灯り、ビルの外からも思わず惹きつけられてしまう。

IGAKUCHO BUILDING 2nd FLOOR GALLERY: Modern Art and Crafts of Niigata

Explore a world of creativity at this unique venue where old-fashioned charm meets modern artistry. The building houses a specialty toy shop, an architect's office, and a design studio. On the second floor, you'll find a rental space for pottery and art exhibitions. The rental room is ideal for showcasing your own exhibition if you're an artist.

加納いずみ
アート好き。学生時代は古町で古着を買い漁っていた。 現在は年に数回作品展示を開催。

95

蔵織のシーズンの企画展
を楽しむ

CD ショップ コンチェルトさんに近況報告に伺うと、毎回必ず何かしら面白い企画展をしているので蔵織さんにも寄っていきます。蔵織さんは、ギャラリーとして個展や演奏会などを開催しながら、新潟の文化・歴史を発信しています。シーズンによりますが、お気に入りは雛人形の展示。大小さまざまな新潟の歴史ある雛人形たちが勢揃いしているのは圧巻です。

Experience the Special Exhibit at GALLERY KURAORI

The Kuraori Gallery in Niigata offers a glimpse into the city's rich cultural heritage. The gallery hosts personal exhibitions and concerts from time to time, showcasing the works of local artists. One of their most popular exhibitions is the Hina-Doll display, which features a collection of historical Hina dolls. These dolls are an integral part of the Japanese Girls' Festival and are displayed in various poses and costumes. The exhibition is a great way to learn about the history and culture of Niigata.

池ヶ谷奏
コンテンポラリーダンサー兼ダンス講師として新潟と東京の 2 拠点で活動中。新潟に来た 12 年前から古町近辺に住んでおり、新しくなっていく店々と変わらない景色を楽しんでいる。

96

Artefakt Coffee & Press の
印刷ギャラリーを観覧する

下町の「吉野活版所」は古町10番、喜ぐちのそば、あの甘納豆の佐藤菓子店の隣です。空き家となっていた歴史的建造物が近い将来壊されてしまうと知り、自ら買い取った konkret 店主のマイク。そこを自家焙煎コーヒーと販売所兼印刷ギャラリーとしてオープンさせました。そしてオリジナルオーダーとしてリソグラフ印刷の注文受付も対応しています。コーヒーを買うのも良し、時間があえばマイクによる大正時代の歴史的建造物の見学ができます。

Printing Gallery at ARTEFAKT COFFEE & PRESS

The Printing Gallery is located in the lower Furumachi area of Niigata and is owned by Mike, who also owns Konkret, a nearby coffee shop. He had learned that the historical building, Yoshino Kappan-jo (Letter Print House), was to be demolished and decided to obtain it. He then opened a roastery and printing gallery in the building. The printing gallery takes orders for lithograph printing. If you visit the gallery and buy some coffee beans, you might be lucky enough to get a tour of this over 100-year-old building from Mike himself!

須貝秀昭
旧中条町出身。高校の時は古町に遊びに行くのがステイタスだった。今は新潟着物男子部部長として毎週のように着物で古町を飲み歩く。

Visit

97

りゅーとぴあで舞台芸術や音楽を鑑賞する

信濃川のすぐそばにある「りゅーとぴあ 新潟市民芸術文化会館」には多種多様なプログラムを行なうことができるスタジオ、劇場、コンサートホール、能楽堂がある。公園のようにふらっと入って、ずらっと並ぶいろいろなプログラムのフライヤーを眺めるだけでもとてもワクワク。コンサートや演劇の帰りに白山神社を通って、古町へ美味しいものを食べに行き、友人たちとコンサートの感想を語らいます。

Enjoy performing arts and music at RYUTOPIA.

Ryutopia is a performing arts center located in Niigata City. It offers various programs and performing arts, including studio, theater, concert hall, and Noh theater. You can walk in freely and look around the flyers about programs and events. After the show, take a walk through Hakusan Shrine and make your way to Furumachi to grab a bite to eat with your pals.

豊島淳子 | BarBookBox
東中通にあるトールビル3階で Book Bar＋Shop「BarBookBox STORE」を経営。古町8番町の洋酒バー カマラードが修行先。

98

古町演芸場で大衆演劇に触れる

泣いて笑える演劇。そして華やかな歌謡ショー。1回のチケットでたっぷり3時間楽しめます。毎月、劇団が変わるので推しを見つけるのも楽しみです。令和4年4月より再開した古町演芸場。場所は古町通6番町。昼の部と夜の部があり、学生さんは学割もあります。近場で大衆演劇を楽しむにはもってこいです。

FURUMACHI ENGEIJO: Theatrical Entertainment in Downtown Furumachi

Enjoy a delightful blend of laughter, tears, and melodious songs. This three-hour entertainment extravaganza awaits you with a single admission. Each month, a fresh traveling theater group graces the stage, so you're sure to discover your favorites. Since resuming operations in April 2023 after the COVID-19 pandemic, they've been lighting up Furumachi 6th Street. Join them for both daytime and evening shows, with special student discounts available. Don't miss the enchanting Taishu Engeki, a showcase of Japanese traditional commoners' life entertainment.

野澤葉子
萬松堂で本を買い、喫茶マキでランチを食べながら読書。

夜の鍋茶屋通で
個性的なお店をまわる

「鮨割烹丸伊」は、家族でも1人でも会社の接待などでも利用できる落ち着いた雰囲気のお店です。近くの「わいんばーあべ」は、新潟には少ないワインバー。有名なワイナリーもあればあまり知られていないワイナリーもあり、いろいろワインを飲みたい人にオススメのお店。ベイクドチーズケーキとオリジナルサワー「あべレモン」が絶品！「BARDOGGIE」は、鍋茶屋通りにひっそりと佇むショットバー。ウイスキーの種類が豊富です（珍しいバーボンもありました）葉巻も吸えるらしいので興味ある方はぜひ。

Go Bar-Hopping on NABEJAYA STREET

Nabejaya Street is a historic street in Niigata, Japan, known for its vibrant nightlife and culinary scene. Check out these restaurants and bars: Sushi Kappo Marui is a quiet restaurant that welcomes families, company parties, or solo customers. They offer a variety of Japanese dishes and sushi. Abe Wine Bar is a cozy wine bar that offers a selection of well-known and lesser-known wines for wine lovers. Their baked cheesecake and original cocktail, Abe Lemon, are must-tries. BARDOGGIE is a shot bar with a wide range of whisky and bourbon. They also offer cigars for those who enjoy smoking.

鈴木太朗

新潟市駅前のホテルに勤務。古町は独特の落ち着いた空気感があります。良いお店がたくさんあるので「もてなす」という空気感が広がった場所だと思っています。

100

寄居浜で日本海に沈む夕陽を眺める

寄居浜から日和浜あたりは海を見渡せ
る公園も整備されていて、子ども達が
遊んでいたり、犬の散歩で足を止めて
海を眺めている方がいたり。私は特に
夕日が沈むあたりから走り、海の向こ
うに見える佐渡の裏手に夕陽が沈むな
んとも美しい様子を見るのが大好きで、

ジョギングコースとして選んでいます。
夕方になるとカップルやご近所のお年
寄りの方やカメラに夕陽をおさめるた
めに来ているような方もたくさん見ら
れそんな様子にもホッコリ。なんて事
ないけど、いい時間が過ごせるのでオ
ススメです。

Enjoy the Sunset at YORII HAMA BEACH

Yorii Hama to Hiyori Hama are beautiful beaches overlooking the Sea of Japan. You can spend a good time with your loved ones, watching the sun go down beyond Sado Island. Children can play around while dog owners can stop to enjoy the sunset. Many couples and local seniors come here for the view. It's a popular photo spot for photographers. You can also start your jogging around the time when the sun starts to shift.

北村美和子 ｜ m.holy
本町５でレディスのセレクトショップを経営。
個性的な小さな店が点在する古町が面白いと感
じ、迷いなく古町エリアでお店をオープン。

Visit

Editor's Note　編集後記

　古町を愛する人たちによる、100通りの古町を集めた『新潟古町100選』がついに完成しました。企画者の古町セッション・近藤潤さんが中心となってクラウドファンディングをスタートしたのが、2023年8月のこと。約1ヶ月の支援期間を経て176％の達成、さらには新潟県を代表する地銀のご支援を乗せて、最終的に210％を達成しました。

　まず、この本を出版できるようにご支援いただいた167名の方、そして諸企業の皆さまに、厚く厚く御礼申し上げます。

　今回出版のチャンスをいただいた私たちは、制作するなかで何度も話し合いを重ね「古町を、どこまで多く遠くの人へ届けられるか」と向き合い続けました。
――古町を知らなかった人が足を運んでくれるきっかけになるだろうか。
――この街をよく知る人にとっても、古町がさらにわくわくできるような本であってほしい。
　さまざまな議論がありながらも、古町を代表する本を作りたいという気持ちをなんとか形にすることができました。制作チームはそれぞれが本業を持っていて、建築家や現代美術家、英語教師、介護士、看護師、場の運営、高校生まで…（！）と、多岐にわたります。本の中では、そんな多様なメンバーだからこその "こだわり" も随所に見られることでしょう。ぜひ、この本を頼りに私たちの愛する古町を巡り、知っていただけたらとても嬉しく思います。

　そして何より、エピソードを寄せてくださった紹介者の皆さんがこれからも引き続き、自分らしく過ごすことのできる大切な古町であれますようにと願っています。

編集者 金澤李花子

Special Supporters

ご支援いただいた方々

 and wood

 第四北越銀行 古町支店

MoAsobiⁱ 太陽交通グループ

近藤哲央 & 初枝　　　　　**髙橋功 & フミ**

佐藤春雄　　　　　　　みぼごん
にいがたいいとこ　　　スズキ経営株式会社

はるにゃん	小林紘大	小松雅人
上古町 SAN	Postmaster	細川敏祐貴
むろはし あい	にわ彌	和 gen
相馬寿成	岡田亮一	お茶のうずまき屋
駒形千夏	レルヒさん	popo
大沢雄城	富沢	五十嵐奈穂子
清水友裕	白石浪	ブルーカフェ
稲葉一樹	もろはしまこと	真島裕也・小百合
寺尾仁＆知香子	たくる	樋熊佑弥
鈴木麻悠子	Atelier Perle	渡辺晴樹
大賀健男	小田昌栄	佐々木明人
村田容子	近藤裕子	桝潟晃広
秋山和幸	こたけなおこ	こいわ
ke-shiki	YAKKOTE堀	マリールゥ
榎並正敏	河村慧	
江部陽貴	宮裡弘樹	ほか、協力者の皆様

Project Team

Planner + Designer	近藤潤	／建築家
Editor	金澤李花子	／編集者
English Translator	小林恵子	／英語インストラクター
	Neal Graham	／英語教師
Photographer	伊藤知香	／看護師
	真保由樹	／介護士
Illustrator	相川恵子	／画家
Promotion Assistant	榎並詩乃	／高校生

新潟古町100選

2024年4月1日　第1刷発行

著　者　　古町セッション
　　　　　〒951-8061 新潟県新潟市中央区西堀通6-876 千歳ビル3B
　　　　　https://furumachisession.com

発行者　　太田宏司郎

発行所　　株式会社パレード
　　　　　大阪本社　〒530-0021　大阪府大阪市北区浮田1-1-8
　　　　　　　　　　TEL 06-6485-0766　FAX 06-6485-0767
　　　　　東京支社　〒151-0051　東京都渋谷区千駄ヶ谷2-10-7
　　　　　　　　　　TEL 03-5413-3285　FAX 03-5413-3286
　　　　　https://books.parade.co.jp

発売元　　株式会社星雲社（共同出版社・流通責任出版社）
　　　　　〒112-0005　東京都文京区水道1-3-30
　　　　　TEL 03-3868-3275　FAX 03-3868-6588

印刷所　　創栄図書印刷株式会社